OAT

No Child Left Behind
A Guide for Professionals

Mitchell L. Yell
University of South Carolina

Erik Drasgow
University of South Carolina

PEARSON
Merrill
Prentice Hall

Upper Saddle River, New Jersey
Columbus, Ohio

061042

Vice President and Publisher: Jeffery W. Johnston
Acquisitions Editor: Allyson P. Sharp
Editorial Assistant: Kathleen S. Burk
Production Editor: Linda Hillis Bayma
Design Coordinator: Diane C. Lorenzo
Cover Design: Ali Mohrman
Production Manager: Laura Messerly
Director of Marketing: Ann Castel Davis
Marketing Manager: Autumn Purdy
Marketing Coordinator: Tyra Poole

Pearson Prentice Hall™ is a trademark of Pearson Education, Inc.
Pearson® is a registered trademark of Pearson plc
Prentice Hall® is a registered trademark of Pearson Education, Inc.
Merrill® is a registered trademark of Pearson Education, Inc.

Pearson Education Ltd.
Pearson Education Singapore Pte. Ltd.
Pearson Education Canada, Ltd.
Pearson Education—Japan

Pearson Education Australia Pty. Limited
Pearson Education North Asia Ltd.
Pearson Educación de Mexico, S.A. de C.V.
Pearson Education Malaysia Pte. Ltd.

10 9 8 7 6 5 4
ISBN: 0-13-118532-2

Dedication

We would like to thank Allyson Sharp, our Merrill/Prentice Hall Editor, for her encouragement and feedback. We also thank Ann Davis, also of Merrill/Prentice Hall, for suggesting this project.

Mitchell Yell would like to thank his wife, Joy, and three sons, Nick, Eric, and Alex for their patience and support.

Erik Drasgow would like to thank his wife, Deanna, and all of his children for their support and Miss Betty Miner, for getting him started on the right path.

Preface

This Merrill/Prentice Hall Student Enrichment Series guide examines the No Child Left Behind Act (NCLB) of 2001 and its effect on the education of students in America's public schools. This law is a reauthorization of the Elementary and Secondary School Act and represents a very significant expansion of the federal government into education. The goal is to acquaint readers with NCLB.

This guide describes the legal structure of NCLB. No Child Left Behind is a massive and complex law that consists of more than 1,000 pages of statutes and regulations. The purpose of the law, with special attention to those sections of the law that are most relevant to schools, is addressed. Important principles of the law relevant to states, school districts, and schools are reviewed, but a comprehensive examination of NCLB is beyond the scope of this guide. For readers seeking more information, additional resources throughout each section are provided.

For readers to gain a thorough understanding of this very important law, they need to know how their state addresses and applies NCLB's requirements. Each state will have its own unique ways of addressing the requirements of the law. Discussion questions throughout each section require the reader to seek information about their state's interpretation of NLCB.

Contents

Chapter 1: The No Child Left Behind Act of 2001: Purpose, Goals, and Structure

And now it's up to you, the local citizens
of America, to stand up and demand higher
standards, and to demand that no child—not
one single child in America—is left behind.

— President George W. Bush,
January 8, 2002

President Bush signed the No Child Left Behind Act (NCLB) of 2001 on January 8, 2002. In a departure from the usual practice of signing bills in the Rose Garden of the White House, President Bush signed the NCLB at a ceremony at Hamilton High School, a public high school in Hamilton, Ohio. President Bush chose Hamilton, Ohio for the signing ceremony because it was the home of Representative John Boehner, Chairman of the House Education Committee.

After signing the bill, President Bush and U.S. Secretary of Education Rod Paige embarked on a daylong tour to participate in ceremonies to celebrate the signing of the law in the home states of Republican Senator Judd Gregg of New Hampshire, Democratic Senator Ted Kennedy of Massachusetts, and Democratic Representative George Miller of California. These two senators and two congressmen had led the bipartisan congressional efforts to pass this legislation. The House and the Senate passed the final version of NCLB by overwhelming margins.

No Child Left Behind is a comprehensive and complex education law that increased federal funding to states by almost 25% from the previous year. The law represents an unprecedented increase in the role that the federal government plays in education because along with the increase in funding, NCLB also increases federal mandates and requirements of states, school districts, and public schools. In fact, NCLB represents the most significant expansion of the federal government into education in our nation's history.

The central mandates of NCLB require states to (a) ensure that highly qualified teachers are in every classroom, (b) use research-based practices as the foundation of instruction, (c) develop tests to assess students so that data-driven decisions become an integral part of the educational system, and (d) hold schools accountable for the performance of all students. When it was passed, Congress and the White House believed that NCLB would significantly alter the manner by which public schools educate our nation's young people.

In this book in the Merrill/Prentice Hall Student Enrichment Series, we examine the NCLB Act of 2001 and its effect on the education of students in America's public schools. Our goal is to familiarize readers with this important law. To do this, we first review the historical developments that led to the passage of the NCLB. Second, we examine the purpose, goals, and structure of the law, because we believe that prior to examining the structure of the NCLB, it is important to understand the purpose of the law. Third, we consider the major principles of NCLB. Next, we analyze the sections of the law that are most directly relevant to parents and educators. In this section, we more closely examine the structure and specific requirements of NCLB. We conclude by offering our thoughts regarding the implications of the NCLB for students, parents, teachers, and administrators.

For More Information

The No Child Left Behind Act is codified at 20 U.S.C. § 6301 et seq. The Statute and a PDF of the law are available online at http://www.ed.gov/policy/elsec/leg/esea02/index.html

The regulations for Title I of No Child Left Behind are codified at 34 C.F.R. § 200 et seq. They are available online at http://www.ed.gov/legislation/FedRegister/finrule/2002-4/120202a.html

---

The Development of the NCLB Federal Involvement in Education

Our nation's system of government is a federal system. This means that the government of the United States is composed of a union of states united under a single central (i.e., federal) government. In this system, the federal government protects the people's rights and liberties and acts to achieve certain ends while simultaneously sharing authority and power with the states. The U.S. Constitution sets forth the nature of this arrangement in the Tenth Amendment. The national government, therefore, has specific powers granted to it in the Constitution and those powers not granted to the national government are the province of the states.

FYI

What is the Tenth Amendment to the U.S. Constitution?

The Tenth Amendment requires that "The powers not delegated to the United States, nor prohibited by it to the states, are reserved to the states respectively, or the people." Because the Constitution does not mention education, it is reserved to the states or to the people. This means that state governments have primary control over education.

The U.S. Constitution does not contain any provisions regarding education. Thus, the federal government has no authority to create a national education system nor can it order states or local school districts to use specific curriculum or adopt particular policies. Instead, the laws of the 50 states govern education.

The federal government's funding role in education has never exceeded approximately 10% of the total amount of money spent on education. Therefore, 90% of all money expended on education is done by states and local school districts. Nevertheless, involvement of the federal government has been an important factor in the progress and growth of education. The federal government's role, however, has been indirect. The earliest method of indirect federal involvement in education was through federal land grants when the federal government provided land to the states for the purpose of creating and aiding the development of public schools. In addition to the land grants creating public schools, Congress provided grants of land in the Morrill Act of 1862 to each state to be used for colleges. In the land grants, the federal government had no direct control of education in the public schools or colleges.

In more recent times, the federal government has continued the indirect assistance to education through categorical grants. The purpose of the categorical grants has been to provide supplementary assistance to the state systems of education and to shape educational policy in the states. States have the option of accepting or rejecting the categorical grants offered by the federal government. If states accept the categorical grants, the states must abide by the federal guidelines for the use of these funds. Examples of categorical grants include the National Defense Education Act of 1958, the Higher Education Facilities Act of 1963, the Vocational Education Act of 1963, the Elementary and Secondary Education Act of 1965, and the Education for All Handicapped Children Act of 1975 (now the Individuals with Disabilities Education Act). The role of the federal government in guiding educational policy has increased greatly through the categorical grants (Alexander & Alexander, 2001). Perhaps the most significant of these early laws was the Elementary and Secondary Education Act (ESEA) of 1965.

The Elementary and Secondary Education Act of 1965

The ESEA of 1965 was passed as part of President Lyndon Johnson's War on Poverty. ESEA appropriated federal money to states to improve educational opportunities for disadvantaged children. Although Congress allocates funds to the ESEA annually, Congress must reauthorize the law every 5 or 6 years.

FYI

What is reauthorization?

When Congress passes statutes that appropriate money they are said to authorize the law. If the law is funded permanently, the funding will continue as long as the law remains unchanged. If a law is funded on a limited basis, the funding period will be designated in the statute. When this period of time expires, Congress has to reauthorize funding or it can let funding expire.

The first part of the ESEA, Title I, was the largest section of the law. The federal government developed a number of formulas to determine which schools would be Title I schools. These formulas involved data such as number of students who were eligible to receive free or reduced lunch or the percentage of students within a school's attendance zone who received public assistance. If either of the two types of data exceeded a poverty cutoff rate, the school was eligible to receive Title I funds. Schools could use these funds to supplement existing services paid for by local funds. The amount of federal money provided to the states fluctuated in the years following passage of the ESEA. The law's basic commitment to assisting states to ensure that equal educational opportunities were provided to economically disadvantaged students, however, has remained unchanged.

A Nation at Risk

During the Reagan administration, the Secretary of Education assembled the Commission on Excellence in Education. In 1983, the Commission issued its report, *A Nation at Risk*. According to the report, the nation's educational system was producing mediocre results, and America's students were falling further and further behind their foreign counterparts. Furthermore, the report called for a commitment to placing education at the top of the nation's agenda. The document was a very important factor in the origin of the current educational reform efforts.

One of the recommendations in the report was that schools needed to adopt higher and measurable standards for academic performance. States began work on establishing academic standards for student achievement, and by 1990 the National Center for Education Statistics reported that nearly 40% of high school students met the academic standards that were recommended in *A Nation at Risk*.

For More Information

The archived report, *A Nation at Risk*, can be found at http://www.ed.gov/pubs/NatAtRisk/risk.html

---

The National Education Summit

In 1989, President George H. W. Bush convened the 50 governors as part of the first National Education Summit. The governors reached consensus regarding the state of education in America and the need for a national strategy to address the problems with public school education. As a result of this summit, six educational goals were developed that were to be achieved by the year 2000. These educational goals became part of President Bush's education legislation, America 2000.

President Bill Clinton made many of these goals the centerpiece of his Goals 2000: Educate America Act. This act created the National Education Standards and Improvement Council. This council had the authority to approve or reject academic standards that were developed by states. Because of opposition in Congress, the commission eventually was disbanded.

The Improving America's Schools Act of 1994

The federal role in government, however, continued with the passage of the Improving America's Schools Act (IASA) of 1994. This law was a reauthorization and revision of the ESEA. The central purpose of IASA was to implement standards-based education throughout the nation. In essence, IASA created a new framework for the federal role in elementary and secondary education, in which the federal government not only provided aid to schools serving economically disadvantaged students but extended federal support to the states' implementation of local and state standards-based reform. The IASA was based on states' developing challenging academic standards, creating and aligning assessments for all students, holding schools accountable for results, and increasing aid to high-poverty schools (Cohen, 2002). In fact, many of the requirements introduced in IASA were revised by and retained in the NCLB (e.g., content standards, assessments, adequate yearly progress). Although states were able to develop their own system for addressing IASA requirements, they had to meet the requirements of the law to receive federal funds.

For More Information

Legislation, regulations, and policy guidance for programs still being implemented under the IASA are available at http://www.ed.gov/about/offices/list/oese/legreg.html?exp=0

The No Child Left Behind Act of 2001

When President George W. Bush took office, he announced that NCLB was the number one priority of his administration's domestic agenda. No Child Left Behind reauthorized the ESEA and also built on the foundation laid in IASA by including significant changes to the federal government's role in education. The most significant change was to require that all public schools bring every public school student up to state standards in reading and math within a certain period of time, thus closing the achievement gap based on race, ethnicity, and language (Cohen, 2002). An overwhelming bipartisan majority in both the House and the Senate passed the NCLB legislation. (The final version of the NLCB passed by a vote of 381 to 41 in the House and 87 to 10 in the Senate.) The NCLB increased federal spending on education by almost 25%. The law also significantly increased federal requirements and mandates on the states.

Summary of the Federal Role in Education

Education is primarily a local and state responsibility. States and school districts provide approximately 90% of the funding. They determine attendance, enrollment, graduation requirements, and develop curricula. Thus, the federal contribution to education is about 10%. Despite the low level of funding, the federal government's role in education has been an important one. This is because the federal government provides funds to assess states in critical areas such as education of economically disadvantaged children.

In 1965, Congress passed the Elementary and Secondary Education Act, which initiated a number of programs that focused on providing federal aid to assist states in providing educational programs for poor children. Congress has reauthorized this law a number of times. The two most recent reauthorizations to the Elementary and Secondary Education Act were the Improving America's Schools Act of 1994 and the No Child Left Behind Act of 2001. The purposes of these two laws were to (a) continue the federal government's commitment to ensuring equal access to education for poor and disadvantaged students, (b) promote educational excellence for all of America's students, and (c) hold schools accountable for the performance of its students. Since the publication of *A Nation at Risk* in 1983, the federal government has increased efforts to hold schools accountable for achieving educational results. These efforts, which required an increase in the role of the federal government in education, led to the passage of NCLB.

The following section examines the purpose, goals, and structure of the major principles of NCLB.

For More Information

To find out more about the federal government's role in education, go to http://www.ed.gov/about/overview/fed/role.html?src=ln

This U.S. Department of Education web page discusses the role of the Department, its mission, and staffing.

The Purpose, Goals, and Structure of No Child Left Behind

No Child Left Behind makes significant changes in the federal government's involvement in education and in the ways that schools will educate children in American schools. In this book, we will examine this law and how, in its few years of existence, it is affecting public education. Prior to examining the content of NCLB, however, it is important to understand the purpose, goals, and structure of the law.

The Purpose of No Child Left Behind

The primary purpose of NCLB is to ensure that students in every public school achieve important learning goals while being educated in safe classrooms by well-prepared teachers. To increase student achievement, the law requires that school districts assume responsibility for ensuring that all its students reach 100% student proficiency levels within 12 years on tests assessing important academic content. Furthermore, NCLB requires schools to close academic gaps between economically advantaged students and students who are from different economic, racial, and ethnic backgrounds as well as students with disabilities.

To measure progress, NCLB requires that states administer tests to all public school students. The states set proficiency standards, called adequate yearly progress, that progressively increase the percentage of students in a district that must meet the proficiency standard. If a school

8

district does not meet these proficiency levels, the law mandates that sanctions and corrective actions be applied.

No Child Left Behind has required a major shift in the ways that teachers, administrators, and state department of education personnel think about public schooling. No Child Left Behind is a very controversial law because to a greater degree than ever before, educators are under growing pressure to increase achievement of all students, to narrow the test score gap between different groups of students, and to ensure that all teachers are highly qualified (Anthes, 2002). Moreover, educators will now be held responsible for bringing about these changes. In commenting on the effect that NCLB will have on school leaders, the Education Commission of the States (Anthes, 2002) noted that:

> Today, expectations for (school leaders) run well beyond managing budgets and making sure the buses run on time. They are counted on to be the instructional leaders of their schools and districts: to understand effective instructional strategies, regularly coach and observe classroom teachers, and be able to analyze student achievement data to make more effective instructional decisions. The (NCLB) puts more pressure on the public education system to increase student achievement for all students. (p. 1)

The Goals of No Child Left Behind

The primary goals of NCLB are as follows:

- All students will achieve high academic standards, by attaining proficiency or better, in reading and mathematics by the 2013-2014 school year.

- Highly qualified teachers will teach all students by the 2005-2006 school year.

- All students will be educated in schools and classrooms that are safe, drug free, and conducive to learning.

- All limited English proficient students will become proficient in English.

- All students will graduate from high school.

These goals will pose great challenges for schools, school districts, and states. No Child Left Behind requires states to test students to ensure that these goals will be met, and it holds schools, school districts, and states accountable for making demonstrable improvements toward meeting these goals. In an effort to assist states to achieve these goals, Congress significantly increased federal spending on education and gave states greater flexibility to use federal funds in ways that will be of the greatest benefit to individual school districts. Although we may debate about how realistic these goals are, and many have, we can all agree that these goals will require a fundamental change in the ways that we measure student progress.

The Structure of No Child Left Behind

To achieve these goals, Congress created a massive and complex law. No Child Left Behind is composed of 10 titles or sections. Each of these titles contains a number of parts and subparts. These titles and parts are listed in Table 1.

Table 1: No Child Left Behind

Title		Parts
I.	Improving the Academic Achievement of the Disadvantaged	• Improving Basic Programs • Student Reading Skills Improvement Grants • Education of Migratory Children • Prevention and Intervention Programs for Neglected, Delinquent, or At-Risk Children • National Assessment of Title I • Comprehensive School Reform • Advanced Placement Programs • School Dropout Prevention • General Provisions
II.	Preparing, Training, and Recruiting High Quality Teachers and Principals	• Teacher and Principal Training and Recruiting Fund • Mathematics and Science Partnerships • Innovation for Teacher Quality • Enhancing Education Through Technology
III.	Language Instruction for Limited English Proficient and Immigrant Students	• English Language Acquisition Act • Improving Language Instruction Education • General Provisions
IV.	21st Century Schools	• Safe and Drug-Free Schools and Communities • 21st Century Learning Centers • Environmental Tobacco Smoke
V.	Promoting Informed Parental Choice and Innovative Programs	• Innovative Programs • Public Charter Schools

11

		• Magnet Schools Assistance
		• Fund for the Improvement of Education
VI.	Flexibility and Accountability	• Improving Academic Achievement
		• Rural Education Initiative
		• General Provisions
VII.	Indian, Native Hawaiian, and Alaskan Native Education	• Indian Education
		• Native Hawaiian Education
		• Alaska Native Education
VIII.	Impact Aid Program	
IX.	General Provisions	• Definitions
		• Flexibility in the Use Funds
		• Coordination of Programs
		• Waivers
		• Uniform Provisions
		• Unsafe School Choice Option
X.	Repeals, Redesignations, and Amendments to Other Statutes	• Repeals
		• Redesignations
		• Homeless Education
		• Native American Education Improvement
		• Higher Education Act of 1965
		• General Education Provisions Act
		• Miscellaneous Other Statutes

Every element of this structure is intended to move all public school students progressively closer to the overall levels of proficiency set by their respective states. Although all 10 titles have important content, the first 7 titles will have the greatest significance for teachers, principals, and parents. Therefore, we will concentrate on these titles in this book. Rather than going through the titles line by line, however, we will explain the significance of each of these sections.

12

The next section examines the major principles of NCLB.

The Major Principles of NCLB

No Child Left Behind consists of four overarching principles: accountability for results, an emphasis on using research-based instruction, expanded local control and flexibility, and expanded parental options. These four principles are woven throughout every aspect of the law.

Accountability for Results

No Child Left Behind focuses on (a) increasing the academic performance of all public school students, and (b) improving the performance of low-performing schools. It does this by requiring states and school districts to identify each child and group of children and to measure their progress every year. The results of these measures are then reported to parents. This information provides parents with data about where their child stands academically and if their child's school and school district are succeeding in meeting state standards. Thus, these assessments are also used to hold schools accountable for the achievement of all students.

To receive federal funding under NCLB, states must submit accountability plans to the U.S. Department of Education. These plans must detail the state's procedures for reporting school performance and their system for holding schools and school districts accountable for increasing student achievement. In accordance with the terms of NCLB, states must develop academic standards and tests to assess students' knowledge and skills in reading and math in grades 3 through 8. Furthermore, states must set state proficiency standards as goals that schools and school districts must attain within certain periods of time. These proficiency standards are academic goals that detail what every child should know and learn.

The purpose of the state tests is to enable stakeholders (e.g., teachers, administrators, parents, policymakers, and the general public) to understand and compare the performances of schools against the standards for proficiency as set by the states. Additionally, test data are disaggregated and reported for students who are economically disadvantaged, disabled, limited English proficient, as well as by race and ethnicity. The purpose of disaggregation by subgroups of students is to ensure that schools will be responsible for improving the achievement of *all* of their students. The purpose of this reporting requirement is to ensure that no subgroup of students is excluded from the states' accountability systems. Schools also are required to issue annual report cards to the public, which will provide stakeholders with information that will allow them to compare performances of schools against the state standards. Thus, stakeholders will be able to hold schools accountable for improving student achievement.

States develop a definition, called adequate yearly progress (AYP), to use each year to determine if schools and school districts are meeting the state standards quickly enough to enable them to have 100% of their students proficient on the academic standards within 12 years. The AYP is the minimum level of improvement that schools must achieve each year. Regulations to NCLB included guidelines to assist states in defining AYP. Individual schools that do not meet AYP are designated "low performing."

If schools and school districts meet or exceed state proficiency standards they will be eligible to receive academic achievement awards. These rewards, which are determined by each state, often consist of public commendations and recognition. If schools and school districts do not make sufficient yearly progress toward meeting state proficiency goals, they will be given assistance by the state. This assistance consists of the development of specific plans that use research-based strategies to enable the school to address the academic achievement problems that caused it to be identified. If schools still fail to progress they will be subject to corrective action that may consist of replacing school staff and implementing a new curriculum. If this doesn't work, schools may eventually face restructuring.

Research-Based Instruction

Too often, schools have used program and practices based on fads, fancy, and personal bias, which have proven to be ineffective. Unfortunately, when ineffective procedures are used, it is at the expense of students. No Child Left Behind emphasizes using educational programs and practices that have been demonstrated to be effective by rigorous scientific research. This means that there is reliable evidence that a program works.

In the past few years, there have been a number of national efforts to ensure that teachers across the nation use instructional procedures that have been validated as effective by scientific research. For example, the National Research Council (2002) and the Coalition for Evidence-Based Policy (2002) issued reports stating that education will see progress only if educators build a knowledge base of educational practices that rigorous research has proven effective. A central principle in NCLB requires that federal funds be expended to support only those educational activities that are backed by scientifically-based research.

For More Information

To find out more about research-based instruction, go to http://www.excelgov.org/displayContent.asp?Keyword=prppcEvidencel

This page links to the Coalition for Evidence-Based Policy report titled "Bringing Evidence-Driven Progress to Education: A Recommended Strategy for the U.S. Department of Education." The report is available in PDF format. The page also links to a policy forum titled "Rigorous Evidence: The Key to Progress in Education? Lessons from Medicine, Welfare, and Other Fields."

The National Research Council's report on research-based instruction is: National Research Council. (2002). *Scientific research in education.* Center for Education, Division of Behavioral and Social Sciences and Education. Washington, DC: National Academy Press.

Rod Paige, Secretary of the U.S. Department of Education, noted that the intent of NCLB is to require that rigorous standards be applied to educational research and that research-based instruction is used in classroom settings (Paige, 2002). Furthermore, he asserted that states must pay attention to this research and ensure that teachers use evidence-supported methods in classrooms. Paige further stated that NCLB demands the use of methods that really work, "no fads, not feel-good fluff, but instruction that is based upon sound scientific research" (Paige, p. 1). No Child Left Behind targets federal funds to support programs and teaching methods that have actually improved student achievement.

For example, states must ensure that funds for Reading First activities go only to programs that are based on sound scientific research.

What constitutes sound scientific research? The National Research Council (2002) reports that for a research design to be scientific, it must allow for direct, experimental investigation of important educational questions. No Child Left Behind defines scientifically-based research as "research that applies rigorous, systematic, and objective procedures to obtain relevant knowledge" (NCLB § 1208(6)). This includes research that (a) uses systematic, empirical methods that draw on observation or experiment, (b) involves rigorous data analyses that are adequate to state hypotheses and justify the conclusions, (c) relies on measurement or observational methods that provide valid data evaluators and observers and across multiple measures and observations, and (d) has been accepted by a peer-reviewed journal or approved by a panel of independent experts through a comparably rigorous, objective, and scientific review.

For More Information

In 2002, the U.S. Department of Education's Institute of Education Sciences established the "What Works Clearinghouse" to provide a central, independent, and trusted source of scientific evidence on what works in education. All of the research collected by the clearinghouse will be available at its web site http://www.w-w-c.org/

Information on the Department's Institute of Education Sciences is available at http://www.ed.gov/about/offices/list/ies/index.html

---

Local Control and Flexibility

The third major principle of NCLB, local control, allows states and schools greater flexibility and control over how they use the federal education funds. The philosophy behind local control is that school districts and state officials have a greater understanding of their needs than federal officials have, thus, school districts and state officials should have greater flexibility in deciding how to spend their money. For example, school districts can now transfer up to 50% of the federal funds that they receive under a number of programs (i.e., Improving Teacher Quality State Grants, Educational Technology, Innovative Programs, and Safe and Drug-Free Schools) to any of these programs or to Title I programs without having to first get federal approval. Thus, school districts will be able to use funds to address their unique needs.

No Child Left Behind also creates school district and state demonstration programs that will allow certain districts and states to consolidate the funds that they receive under federal education programs. These funds can be used for helping school districts to make adequate yearly progress and narrowing achievement gaps.

Parental Options

If students attend low-performing schools that do not improve within the amount of time specified in the state proficiency goals, parents are given a number of options regarding their child's education. If a school has failed to meet state proficiency goals for 2 consecutive years, parents may elect to have their children transferred to a better-performing public school within their school district. If parents make this choice, then the school district must provide transportation. If a school has failed to meet state proficiency goals for 3 years, children are eligible to receive supplemental educational services such as tutoring and after-school instruction. Additionally, if a school is unsafe or dangerous, or if a student has been a victim of a violent crime while at school, parents may also elect to send their child to a safe school within their school district. The philosophy behind increasing parental options is that these options may help to increase student achievement while simultaneously providing an incentive for the low-performing school to improve. If low-performing schools do not improve, they will lose students and may be subject to restructuring.

Summary of the Major Principles of No Child Left Behind

Four major principles are the foundation of NCLB: (a) making schools, school districts, and states accountable for results; (b) ensuring that research-based instruction is used in our nation's public schools; (c) increasing local control and flexibility in using federal education money; and (d) giving parents public school choice when a school is designated low performing. Congress believed that for too long federal education money had been spent with no clear result. By passing a law based on these principles, Congress believed that parents would be empowered by knowing their child's strengths and weaknesses and how well schools are performing, and teachers and principals would have the information they need to strengthen their programs.

In the following chapters, we will explain the sections of NCLB that are most pertinent to teachers, administrators, and parents.

For More Information

To find out more about the purpose, goals, structure, and principles of No Child Left Behind, go to http://www.ed.gov/nclb/landing.jhtml

This is the U.S. Department of Education's official web site on No Child Left Behind. The web site also links to No Child Left Behind: A Desktop Reference (Microsoft Word or PDF document). A hardcopy of this publication can be ordered online at http://www.edpubs.org/webstore/Content/search.asp (put "No Child Left Behind: A Desktop Reference" in keyword/title box and press go)

The web site also links to a user-friendly guide to No Child Left Behind, the "Teachers Toolbox," which is available in PDF or Word format at http://www.ed.gov/teachers/nclbguide/index2.html

The official web site also links to an online newsletter on No Child Left Behind, "The Achiever." Readers can subscribe to this free newsletter and get back issues at http://www.ed.gov/news/newsletters/achiever/index.html

---

Discussion Questions

1. Explain the role of the federal government in education.

2. How is the No Child Left Behind Act a logical culmination of the federal government into the educational affairs of states that began in 1983 with the publication of *A Nation at Risk*?

3. What is the purpose of the No Child Left Behind Act?

4. Explain the major principles of No Child Left Behind.

Chapter 2: No Child Left Behind: Standards, Assessments, and Accountability

The No Child Left Behind Act sets a clear objective for American education. Every child in every school must be performing at grade level in the basic subjects that are the key to all learning, reading and math. This ambitious goal is the most fundamental duty of every school, and it must, and it will be fulfilled.

— President George W. Bush, June 10, 2002

The President and Congress believed that many schools operate without a clear set of expectations of what students should achieve in important academic subjects. In the NCLB, therefore, states are required to establish their own standards of what students should know and be able to do. Specifically, the NCLB required states to develop academic standards for all students in reading-language arts, math, and science. Additionally, states are free to develop standards in other areas. For example, a state could develop standards in social studies, although social studies standards are not required by the NCLB.

The goal of the NCLB is that every child will be able to demonstrate proficiency on state-defined education standards in reading-language arts, math, and science by the end of the 2013-2014 school year. To reach this goal, all states have developed achievement standards and assessments to measure students' progress toward meeting these standards. Moreover, NCLB requires that states hold schools and school districts accountable for results. This means that every public school and school district in a state must ensure that all students meet the state-defined proficiency levels on their academic standards. If schools or school districts do not meet the required proficiency levels, states are required to provide technical assistance and eventually to apply sanctions (e.g., allowing parents public school choice, requiring schools to pay for supplemental educational services, removing school staff responsible for school problems) to schools that are in need of improvement.

The NCLB provides federal money to assist states in their efforts. To receive federal aid through the NCLB, states are required to submit accountability plans delineating their standards and assessments to the U.S. Department of Education. The next section examines NCLB's requirements regarding standards and assessments.

For More Information

To view states' NCLB accountability plans, go to "Approved state accountability plans" at http://www.ed.gov/admins/lead/account/stateplans03/index.html

Standards

The purpose of the state-defined standards is to provide guidelines to schools, parents, and communities that outline what achievement will be expected of all students. To reach the goal of having every child proficient on state-defined standards by the target date, the NCLB requires every state to develop achievement standards or benchmarks for all public students.

According to the NCLB regulations, state content standards must (a) describe what students will be able to know and do, (b) include coherent and rigorous content standards, and (c) encourage the teaching of advanced skills. Moreover, these standards must be applied equally to all public schools and to all elementary and secondary students. For elementary students, the standards can be grade specific or cover more than one grade. For secondary students, the standards must define the knowledge and skills that all high school students will be expected to demonstrate by the time they graduate.

The NCLB regulations also require that states describe achievement levels to determine how well students are mastering the content standards. States must describe at least three levels of achievement. At minimum, these levels must include a high or advanced level, a proficient level, and a basic level. The advanced and proficient levels describe how well students are mastering the content standards, and the basic level describes how lower achieving students are progressing toward mastering the content standards. The achievement levels also include a description of the competencies associated with each of the content areas for all three levels. The purpose of the achievement levels is to provide information to parents and educators about the progress of students toward meeting the content standards.

Proficiency levels are defined by each state. States are required to implement an assessment system that differentiates among the students at the various proficiency levels. States have the flexibility to define more than three levels of achievement. For example, South Carolina has four levels of achievement (see Table 2).

Table 2: Proficiency Levels from South Carolina

Below Basic: The student has not met minimum expectations for student performance based on the state-adopted curriculum standards.

Basic: The student has met minimum expectations for student performance based on state-adopted curriculum standards.

Proficient: The student has met expectations for student performance based on state-adopted curriculum standards.

Advanced: The student has exceeded expectations for student performance based on state-adopted curriculum standards.

Assessment

The NCLB requires that states implement a statewide assessment system that is aligned to the state standards in reading-language arts, math, and eventually science. The purpose of the statewide testing is to measure how successfully students are learning what is expected of them and how they are progressing toward meeting these important academic standards. All public schools must participate in the statewide assessment by testing 95% of their students. This includes testing at least 95% percent of students in each subgroup (i.e., students from racial and ethnic minority status, and students who are economically disadvantaged, disabled, and limited English proficient). However, if a school has a subgroup that is too small to be statistically significant, they do not have to disaggregate this subgroup's test scores. Students' test scores must be reported in terms of achievement levels on the standards (e.g., advanced, proficient, basic).

States must assess reading-language arts and math annually in grades 3 through 8 and once between grades 10 and 12 by the 2005-2006 school year. Science assessments are required by the 2006-2007 school year for these same grade spans. States have the option of testing in other academic areas, although they are not required to do so. Table 3 contains the NCLB requirements regarding statewide testing.

Table 3: Statewide assessment systems must:

- be used to measure all public school students,

- be valid and accessible for use with the widest range of students,

- be valid, reliable, and consistent with professional and technical standards,

- be objective measures of student achievement, knowledge, and skills and not evaluations of personal or family beliefs and attitudes,

- be designed to provide a coherent system across grades and subjects,

- be designed to produce individual descriptive and diagnostic student reports, and

- enable individualized score analysis to be reported to schools and school districts.

Furthermore, the states are to use the assessment system as the primary means of measuring whether students in public school districts and public schools are making academic improvements. Additionally, this information can be used to identify strengths and weaknesses within the educational system and to help the school district and state to allocate resources to best promote student achievement.

These tests must be administered to all students in public schools in each state. Testing includes students with disabilities and students

23

with limited English proficiency. The next section describes the special accommodations that may be used for testing these two subgroups of students.

Students with Disabilities

The NCLB also requires that school districts provide students with disabilities access to appropriate accommodations if necessary to take the statewide assessment. Students with disabilities are to be held to the standards for the grade in which the student is enrolled, although in some situations, accommodations or modifications may be needed to get a true picture of a student's achievement.

To receive these accommodations or modifications, students with disabilities must be eligible for special education services under the Individuals with Disabilities Education Act (IDEA) or Section 504 of the Rehabilitation Act. Each student's individualized education program (IEP) or 504 planning team must determine if a student can take the statewide assessment without accommodations or modifications, with appropriate accommodations and modifications, or if they will take an alternate assessment. Scores on the statewide assessment, with or without accommodations, or scores on the alternate assessment must be included in all statewide assessment reports. School districts also have to report the percentage of students taking an alternate assessment.

Students with significant cognitive disabilities may be administered alternate assessments if the student's IEP team determines that they cannot participate in all or part of the state assessment. Furthermore, students' scores on these alternate assessments may be included in the state and school district calculations of AYP as long as they do not exceed 1% of all students being tested. The NCLB regulations do not define significant cognitive disabilities; therefore, states are free to develop their own guidelines for IEP teams to follow when determining if a student's disability requires that he or she be given an alternate assessment.

Accommodations, Modifications, and Alternate Assessments

Assessment accommodations are changes in testing materials or procedures that enable a student to participate in an assessment so that his or her abilities, rather than disabilities, are assessed (Thurlow, Elliott, & Ysseldyke, 2003). Accommodations level the playing field for students with disabilities (Elliott & Thurlow, 2000).

Examples of accommodations may include (a) taking a test individually or in a small group instead of a large group, (b) taking more frequent breaks during testing, (c) taking a Braille edition of the test, or (d) marking directly in a response booklet rather than bubbling in answers on a test sheet.

There will be situations when a student with disabilities may be unable to participate in the state assessment. When a student cannot participate, even with accommodations, an alternate assessment serves as a way to gather information needed to measure and document the results of the student's education (Thurlow et al., 2003).

Students with Limited English Proficiency

Students with limited English proficiency (LEP) must be included in the statewide assessments. These statewide assessments must be valid and reliable, may include reasonable accommodations, and when possible, must be in a language and form that is most likely to provide accurate data about the students' knowledge and skills in all subjects with the exception of English. Examples of accommodations for students with LEP may include (a) native-language assessments, (b) extra time, (c) small-group administration, (d) audiotaped instructions in the native language, or (e) the use of dictionaries.

Annual assessments in a student's native language may continue until the student has achieved English proficiency. In most cases, students with LEP who have attended school in the United States, except in Puerto Rico, for 3 consecutive years must be assessed in reading-language arts by using tests written in English.

State accountability plans must confirm that local school districts annually assess students with LEP in their English oral language, reading, and writing skills. The plans also must contain annual measurable objectives to monitor the progress of students with LEP in attaining English proficiency. If a school district fails to meet these objectives for 4 years, the state must require the district to modify its curriculum or its method of instruction.

National Assessment of Educational Progress

The NCLB also requires that every other year, states must administer the fourth- and eighth-grade reading and math tests of the National Assessment of Educational Progress (NAEP) to a random sample of students. Because the statewide reading and math tests will be given each year, the purpose of states' participation in NAEP is to obtain a national comparison of the statewide assessment test. Thus, the comparison of the NAEP to the states' tests can be used to confirm the rigor of the statewide assessment. Additionally, the NAEP-statewide test comparison will let the U.S. Department of Education and the states know how each state is doing when compared to other states and how each state is progressing.

What is the National Assessment of Educational Progress (NAEP)?

NAEP is known as the nation's report card. It is a nationally representative and continuous assessment of American students' knowledge and skills. NAEP is an extensive data collection system that includes achievement tests in a number of areas, including reading and math (Reckase, 2002). NAEP does not provide individual student or school scores. Instead NAEP provides information about subject matter achievement, characteristics of the student population, instructional experiences, and characteristics of the school environment for populations of students.

There is a national NAEP and a state NAEP. The national NAEP reports information for (a) the nation, (b) specific regions of the country, (c) students (e.g., eighth-grade students), and (d) specific subgroups of students (e.g., Asian/Pacific Islander students). The information reported includes student achievement in grades 4, 8, and 12 and is drawn from public and private schools. The state NAEP provides information to states regarding the performance of students in their state. The NAEP assessments are also designed to give information about long-term trends in the basic achievement of students in America's schools.

For More Information

For more information on NAEP, readers are referred to the Nation's Report Card web site at http://nces.ed.gov/nationsreportcard/

Reporting Requirements

The NCLB requires that states use the assessments to produce reports that interpret statewide test results for each student so that teachers, administrators, and parents can understand and address the specific academic needs of each student. This requirement means that the results of the tests must be reported to parents in a format that enables them to understand their child's educational needs and track his or her progress.

When reporting assessment results, states must disaggregate (i.e., separate) the data and report it by subgroups of students. The disaggregated data must be reported by major racial and ethnic groups, English language proficiency status, disability status, migrant status, gender, and economic status. If the number of these students is not sufficient to yield statistically reliable information, however, assessment results do not have to be reported. The purpose of disaggregating data by subgroup is to make sure that no students fall through the cracks. School districts are responsible for ensuring that all students, including students in the subgroups, meet the states' proficiency standards.

States and school districts must issue annual report cards to the public. The purpose of these cards is to report the results of the statewide assessment to the public. States must develop two types of reports: (a) state report cards, and (b) school district report cards. States are free to develop their own report cards; however, they must contain the federally required information listed in Table 4.

Table 4: Minimum Requirements for State and School District Report Cards

Type of Report Card	NCLB Required Information
State Report Card	• Information on student achievement aggregated at each proficiency level
	• Information on student achievement disaggregated by race, ethnicity, gender, disability status, English proficiency, and economic disadvantage
	• Comparison between the actual achievement levels of groups of students and the state's annual measurable objectives on each academic assessment
	• Percentage of students not tested, disaggregated by subgroup

- The most recent 2-year trend in student achievement for each grade and subject area

- Information aggregated on other indicators that the state uses to determine adequate yearly progress

- Graduation rates for students, disaggregated by subgroup

- Information on the performance of school districts in making yearly progress, including the number and names of each school identified for school improvement

- Professional qualifications of teachers, the percentage of teachers with emergency or provisional credentials, and the percentage of classes not taught by highly qualified teachers in the aggregate and for schools in the top and bottom quartile in the state

District Report Cards	- The information described above for the state report card as applied to the school district and each school - The number and percentage of schools identified for school improvement and the length of time the schools have been in that category - Information about how students in the district performed on the statewide assessment compared with the state as a whole - The schools that have been identified as in need of improvement - Information regarding how students in each school performed on the statewide assessment and other indicators of adequate yearly progress compared with students in the district and the state as a whole

In addition to the report cards, each state is required to make an annual report to the Secretary of the U.S. Department of Education regarding (a) its progress developing and implementing academic assessments, and (b) student achievement on those assessments. The state also must report information on supplemental service programs, teacher quality, the names of schools in need of improvement, and public school choice.

The NCLB's requirements regarding assessment are substantial; however, the changes in accountability requirements are even more far reaching (Learning First Alliance, 2002). The following section examines these requirements.

Accountability

Perhaps the most stringent and controversial aspect of the NCLB is the law's accountability system. As discussed in an earlier section, the NCLB requires each state to set rigorous academic content standards for every student. Moreover, every year states must assess students' academic achievement and report the results of these tests to the public. The NCLB also requires that states hold schools accountable for the academic progress of their students by ensuring that all students meet a measurable annual objective called adequate yearly progress (AYP), explained in the following section.

Adequate Yearly Progress

The NCLB requires that each state use the annual statewide assessments to measure the academic progress of its students toward meeting the academic standards. States meet these academic standards by defining what constitutes AYP for students in their schools and school districts. The AYP accountability system must (a) be based on the state's academic standards, statewide assessments, and other indicators (e.g., graduation rates, attendance); (b) take into account the achievement of all public elementary and secondary students; (c) be the same accountability system that a state uses for all its students and school districts; and (d) include rewards (e.g., public recognition for schools and districts that meet the AYP) and sanctions (e.g., school districts that don't make AYP for 2 consecutive years must give students the option to transfer to higher performing schools) that the state will use to hold schools and school districts accountable for student achievement and for making AYP. This accountability procedure means that a school's AYP status is judged by the achievement of its students on the state-defined standards.

Starting in the 2001-2002 school year, states will have 12 years to show that 100% of their public school students meet the reading-language arts and math accountability criteria set by the state. This includes students in the following subgroups: economically disadvantaged, major racial and ethnic group, students with disabilities, or students with limited English proficiency. Additionally, gender is considered when meeting the standards. In the accountability plans submitted to the U.S. Department of Education, each state defined the AYP criteria for increasing student achievement to meet the 100% proficiency goal in reading-language arts and math by the 2013-2014 school year.

To ensure that students from all groups are making progress toward reaching the 100% goal by the target date, the state must set specific targets for all students each year in reading-language arts and math. These specific targets are the AYP criteria.

To set AYP criteria, state education officials must establish a starting point for measuring statewide student progress toward meeting proficiency on statewide standards in reading and mathematics. This starting point is the percentage of students in the state who score "proficient" on the statewide test. The state has to go through three steps to choose the starting point. First, they must determine the average percentage of students reaching proficiency in the lowest achieving schools in the state. For example, if only 16% of all students in the lowest performing school district in the state reach proficiency on the statewide test, the state may use the figure of 16% to calculate the starting point. Second, state officials must determine the percentage of students who achieve proficiency in the lowest achieving subgroup in the state. For example, of the disaggregated subgroups, if students with disabilities score the lowest on statewide tests, then students with disabilities will be chosen for calculating the starting point. Third, state officials must compare the proficiency scores of the lowest subgroup score and the lowest school district and then choose the higher score. If, for instance, the students with disabilities' subgroup scored 20% and the lowest performing school district scored 16%, then 20% (i.e., the higher of the two scores) becomes the starting point or baseline for calculating AYP.

31

Once the starting point is established, the state gradually increases the percentage of students each year that must score at the proficient level so the state reaches the goal of having 100% of their students scoring at the proficient level by 2013-2014. States usually increase the required percentage of students who must be proficient in small increments each year. This annual increase is the measurable annual objective for each year, or AYP.

Figure 1 depicts an example of how AYP is calculated. In this example, assume that the baseline level in 2001-2002 for the state was that 20% of students were proficient in reading-language arts and math tests as measured by the statewide assessment. Because 100% of the state's students and subgroups of students must be proficient in reading-language arts by 2013-2014, the state sets the AYP at slightly higher levels each year (e.g., 3%, 5%) so that the goal is met by the target date. To meet AYP, the required percentage of a school's students must achieve the target level each year on the statewide test in each year. In this example, only 20% of the students reached the proficient level in the 2001-2002 school year. The difference between the current 20% and the goal of 100% is 80%. When the 80% increase is divided by the number of 12 years until the state, school district, or school must reach the goal, the result is an approximately 7% increase each year.

In this example the AYP for the 2004-2005 academic year is 40%. If 40% of a school's students, including students in the disaggregated subgroups, reach the proficient level of 40%, the school has achieved AYP. If, however, 39% or less of a school's students have reached the proficient level, the school has failed to make AYP.

Readers should note that 100% of a state's students must reach 100% proficiency in both reading-language arts and math by the 2013-2014 academic year. In this illustration, only one line is used to depict AYP. When states compute AYP criteria, however, they will usually compute one for reading-language arts and another for math. This is because they may have different starting points and steps to reach 100%.

Figure 1:

Calculating AYP

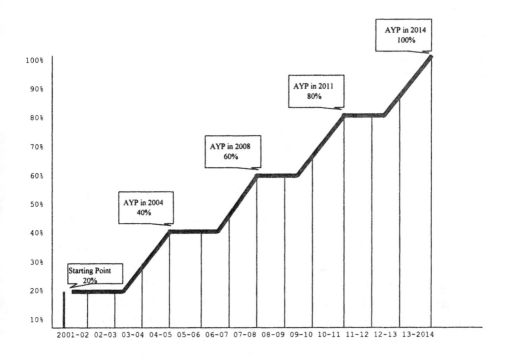

In addition to using assessments to determine AYP, states must use at least one academic measure to show progress. The states can select the indicator at the elementary level, but the indicator must be graduation rates at the secondary level. Schools can meet AYP if each group of students meets or exceeds the state's annual measurable objectives and the school or school district meets the other indicator. For example, if Figure 1 represents the AYP criteria for the years between 2001 and 2013, and a school equals or does better that the AYP in a given year, and they meet the other indicator the state has chosen (e.g., attendance rate), then they have met AYP.

School districts are responsible for measuring the progress of schools in their district, rewarding schools that show substantial improvement, and holding schools accountable when they fail to make AYP as defined by the state. States, in turn, are responsible for ensuring that school districts meet AYP. By the 2004-2005 school year, the U.S.

33

Department of Education will begin reviewing states to determine if the states have met their own definitions of AYP.

The NCLB Act provides a "safe harbor" to avoid over-identifying low-performing schools. In schools where the aggregate group of students makes AYP, but where one or more subgroups fail to make AYP, the school will still make AYP if the following conditions are met: (a) the percentage of students in the subgroup or subgroups who failed to make AYP is reduced by at least 10%, and (b) that group makes progress on one or more of the state's academic indicators. Using Figure 1 as an example, suppose an elementary school gives the statewide assessment to all their students in 2003. The disaggregated data show that the following percentages of students scored "proficient" on the statewide test:

- Students with disabilities – 20% (80% failed to make AYP)
- All students (including all the disaggregated subgroups) – 35%

The AYP cutoff for 2003 is 35%; as a group the entire student body and all the other disaggregated groups scored at a level that meets AYP. However, students with disabilities did not meet the 35% proficiency level. Because all of a school's students and all the disaggregated subgroups must meet 35%, the school will not meet AYP because one of the disaggregated groups, students with disabilities, did not meet AYP.

In 2004, these two groups in the same school make the following scores:

- Students with disabilities – 32% (68% failed to make AYP)
- All students (including all the other disaggregated subgroups) – 45%

The AYP cutoff for 2004 is 40%. Again, as a group, all the school's students, including the other subgroups, exceed the AYP cutoff. Students with disabilities did not make the AYP cutoff; however, the school reduced the percentage of students failing to make AYP by 12% from the previous year. If the school's students with disabilities meet the other AYP indicator set by the state, then the school will make AYP. The school meets the AYP because the students with disabilities made more than a 10% gain from 2003 to 2004, therefore the school reached the safe harbor criteria despite the fact that the students with disabilities subgroup failed to make the required 40%.

What happens when a school makes AYP?

States are responsible for determining its own system of sanctions and rewards to hold all public schools and school districts responsible for meeting AYP. The state may set aside 5% of their Title I funds to provide rewards for the schools and teachers in the schools that (a) substantially close the achievement gap between the lowest and highest performing students, and (b) made outstanding yearly progress for 2 consecutive years. Although each state determines what the rewards will be, rewards often include some form of public recognition and monetary reward. States also can designate schools that have made the greatest achievement gains as "Distinguished Schools."

What happens when a school fails to make AYP?

If a school fails to meet AYP they will receive assistance to improve. The state will designate a school that has not achieved AYP for 2 consecutive years as "identified for improvement." When a school is first identified for improvement, the state provides technical assistance to enable the school to address the specific problems that led to their being identified. The school, in conjunction with parents and outside experts, will develop a two-year improvement plan. Although neither the law not regulations specify who these outside experts may be, probably faculty from institutions of higher education and private consultants who have expertise in research-based strategies in the areas in which the school needs help will qualify as experts.

This technical assistance plan, which must be developed in conjunction with state officials and parents, must address how the school will:

- improve academics,
- incorporate research-based strategies,
- notify and involve parents,
- use 10% of its Title I funds for professional development,
- institute a new teacher mentoring program,
- implement activities outside the regular school day (if necessary).

Moreover, this improvement plan must involve the school's core academic subjects that have the greatest likelihood of raising student achievement so that the school's students meet the proficiency standards.

The statewide testing, therefore, helps schools identify subject areas and teaching procedures that need improvement. For example, if a school meets AYP in math but fails to do so in reading, school officials should target reading for improvement. Officials may decide to adopt a research-based reading curriculum or teaching procedure as a result of the information gained from statewide testing. The school district must help the school develop and implement the plan. Additionally, the school must set aside 10% of its Title I funds for professional development.

The NCLB also has very specific sanctions for schools that do not make AYP. States must determine if each public school and school district achieves AYP, even those schools and districts that do not receive Title I funds. When a school district fails to make AYP, the state must start the corrective actions discussed above. If a school does not make AYP, this information must be published and disseminated to parents, teachers, and the community. The information must be made available in an easy-to-understand format. The next section describes the sanctions that the state will apply to schools and school districts.

If a School Fails to Make AYP for 2 Consecutive Years

The state must continue to provide technical assistance to the school if it fails to make AYP for 2 consecutive years. Additionally, the school must offer the parents of students in the school the option of transferring to another public school within the district. The district must provide the transportation. If a school then makes AYP for 2 consecutive years, the needs improvement designation is removed. If students have chosen to attend another school during this period, they can continue to do so until they finish the top grade in the new school.

No Child Left Behind's Public School Choice Option

An important part of NCLB's accountability requirements is a student's option to transfer from a school that has failed to make AYP for at least 2 consecutive years. If a school has been identified for improvement, corrective action, or restructuring, the school district must give all the school's students the option to transfer to another public school within the district. The students may transfer to a public charter school or a public school within the district, which has not been identified for improvement, corrective action, restructuring, or that is persistently dangerous (see Chapter 5 for a description of when a school is designated "persistently dangerous").

If more than one school within the district meets the NCLB's requirements, the school district must provide parents with a choice of schools. However, NCLB does *not* require the school district to offer the option to attend the specific school that the parent may want.

If a School Fails to Make AYP for 3 Consecutive Years

If a school fails to make AYP for a third consecutive year, the school district will still be obligated to provide technical assistance to the school and to offer school choice. The school also is required to offer supplemental educational services, which may include private tutoring, to low-income (i.e., Title I) students. Schools must provide these supplemental services in addition to instruction during the school day. These services, therefore, may take place before school, after school, on the weekends, or in the summer. Moreover, instruction and supplemental services must be research-based and of high quality. The purpose of the services is to increase the academic achievement of eligible students as measured by the statewide assessment system and thus enable the student to attain proficiency in meeting the state's academic standards.

Parents can choose a provider of these services from a state-approved list. A service provider can be a nonprofit entity, for-profit entity, a local educational agency, an educational service agency, a faith-based organization, or a public school (including a public charter school) as long as it has not been identified for corrective action. Potential providers must meet state selection criteria including (a) having a demonstrated record of effectiveness in increasing the academic achievement of students in subjects relevant to meeting state standards, (b) being capable of providing supplemental educational services that are consistent with the school district's instructional program and the state's standards and achievement requirements, and (c) being financially sound. Additionally, providers must meet the following requirements before they can be added to the state-approved list. The provider must:

- furnish understandable information on a student's progress in increasing achievement to the child's parents and school district;

- ensure that its instruction and content are consistent with the instruction provided and content used by the state and school district;

- ensure that its instruction is aligned with state standards and is secular, neutral, and non-ideological;

- meet all applicable federal, state, and local health, safety, and civil rights laws;

- meet the requirements of a student's IEP, if appropriate;

- require that written parent permission is given before disclosing the identity of any student who is eligible for or receiving services.

When a school district is required to make supplemental services available, they must enter into an agreement with the service provider or providers. This agreement must (a) specify the achievement goals for students, (b) describe how students' progress will be measured, and (c) include a timetable for improving students' achievement. The agreement must also describe procedures for regularly informing a student's parents of his or her progress and how the provider will be paid. Additionally, the school district must implement the plan no later than the beginning of the next school year.

The school district is also required to provide an annual notice to parents about how they may obtain supplemental services and the identity, qualifications, and effectiveness of the providers. The school or school district must assist the parents to choose the provider if requested to do so. When a student receives supplemental services, the school or school district must inform the parent of the student's progress. Table 5 lists requirements regarding supplemental education services.

Table 5: NCLB's Supplemental Educational Services Requirements

Definition and Duties	Requirement
School District Duties	• Provide annual notice to parents concerning how they can obtain supplemental services, including the identity of state-approved providers and a description of the services, qualifications, and effectiveness of the providers.
	• Assist parents in choosing a provider from the state-approved list, if requested to do so by the parents.
	• Apply fair and equitable procedures for serving students if the number of spaces available with approved providers is not sufficient to serve all eligible students whose parents have requested services.
	• Ensure that eligible students with disabilities under the IDEA and Section 504 receive appropriate services that comport with the student's IEP or Section 504 plan.
	• Ensure that LEP students receive appropriate supplemental services.
	• Receive written permission from parents before publicly disclosing the identity of students eligible for services.

If a School Fails to Make AYP for 4 Consecutive Years

If a school fails to make AYP for a fourth consecutive year, the district must continue to (a) provide technical assistance, (b) make supplemental services available, and (c) offer public school choice. Additionally, the school is designated as needing corrective action. These corrective actions, at minimum, must include one of the following actions:

- Replace the school staff members responsible for the school failing to make AYP.

- Implement research-based curriculum, including professional development activities.

- Decrease management authority significantly at the school level.

- Appoint an outside expert to advise the school.

- Extend the school year or school day.

- Restructure the school internally.

If a School Fails to Make AYP After 5 Consecutive Years

If a school fails to meet AYP standards after 1 year of corrective action, which means they have not made AYP for 5 consecutive years, states are required to take corrective actions that involve major restructuring of the school. The restructuring plans should involve one or more of the following changes to the school's governance structure:

- Reopen the school as a public charter school.

- Replace all or most of the school's staff, including the principal, who are responsible for the school's failing to achieve AYP.

- Enter into a contract with an entity, such as a private management company, to operate the school. The company must have demonstrated record of effectiveness.

- Turn over the operation of the school to the state.

- Implement other major restructuring arrangements that are consistent with NCLB.

The school district must continue to provide technical assistance, public school choice, and supplemental education services. Additionally, parents must be notified immediately when a school is identified for restructuring. During the restructuring period, the school must continue to offer parents the option of public school choice and supplemental educational services.

What happens when a school district fails to make AYP?

If an entire school district fails to make AYP, the state takes responsibility for helping the school district develop and implement an improvement plan and for implementing corrective actions. The NCLB requirements regarding the school district's improvement plan and corrective action are the same as the requirements for schools. For example, when a school district is targeted for improvement, they have 3 months to develop or revise an improvement plan. The plan must be developed in consultation with parents, school staff, and other appropriate parties. Additional required components of a school district improvement plan include:

- Measurable goals and targets consistent with the AYP requirements.

- Extended learning time strategies.

- Outlined school district and state responsibilities.

- Efforts to promote effective parental involvement.

The school district must implement the improvement plan no later than the beginning of the school year after it has been identified in need of improvement.

If the entire school district does not achieve AYP for 4 years, the state must implement corrective action, which may include one of the following:

- Deferring programming funds or reducing funds for administration.

- Implementing a new research-based curriculum along with professional development activities.

- Replacing school district personnel.

- Establishing an alternative governance structure.

- Appointing a receiver or trustee to administer the school district in place of the superintendent and school board.

- Abolishing or restructuring the school district.

41

The state may also authorize students in the school district to transfer to higher performing public schools.

What happens when a state fails to make AYP?

The U.S. Department of Education will establish a peer review process to determine whether states are making their AYP goals. If a state fails to make AYP, they will be listed in an annual report to Congress. If a state fails to make AYP for 2 consecutive years, the U.S. Department of Education will provide technical assistance to the state.

Summary of the Assessment and Accountability Provisions of No Child Left Behind

The NCLB requires public schools, public school districts, and states to improve student achievement and close academic achievement gaps among various subgroups of students. It does this by requiring states to develop (a) academic standards in reading-language art, math, and science for all public school students, and (b) assessments to evaluate student progress toward meeting these standards. The annual statewide assessments are must be aligned to the state academic standards and describe at least three achievement levels that measure students' progress toward meeting these academic standards. These levels must include two levels that indicate good achievement toward the standards, advanced and proficient, and one level that indicates inadequate progress toward the standards.

The statewide assessment system is used to hold school districts and schools accountable for ensuring that these academic achievement standards are met. Every public school must make adequate yearly progress toward having 100% of students in the school proficient in state-defined achievement standards by the 2013-2014 school year. The NCLB contains provisions that require states to (a) reward school districts that make progress toward this goal, (b) provide help for public schools and school districts that are not making adequate progress toward this goal, and (c) take corrective actions in school districts that persistently fail to improve.

Important Dates

2002-2003 School Year

✓ States and school districts must issue report cards.

✓ States must set AYP starting points based on 2001-2002 data.

✓ School districts must assess their students with limited English proficiency for their English proficiency.

✓ All states must participate in the fourth- and eighth-grade reading and math NAEP tests.

2005-2006 School Year

✓ States must have science standards.

✓ States must have their annual statewide assessments for reading and math in grades 3 though 8.

2007-2008 School Year

✓ States must have their annual science assessments for grades 3-5, 6-9, and 10-12.

2013-2014 School Year

✓ 100% of public school students in states must meet state proficiency standards in reading and math.

Discussion Questions

Questions—State Standards

1. What are the challenging standards your state has adopted?

2. What are your state's expectations for proficiency? Are they ambitious standards?

Questions—AYP

1. What are your state's baseline scores for determining AYP?

2. What additional elements (e.g., graduation rates, attendance) does your state use to evaluate the quality of schools?

3. How were your state's cut scores determined? What are they?

Questions—Annual Testing

1. Are your state's assessments linked to its standards?

2. Has your state evaluated the technical quality (i.e., reliability and validity) of its assessments?

3. What are your state's policies with respect to testing limited English proficient students on the statewide assessment?

4. What are your state's policies with respect to testing students with disabilities on the statewide assessment?

Questions—State Report Cards

1. What information and measures are included in your state and local report cards?

2. Does your state have an adequate data management system to collect, analyze, and report information collected for the annual report cards?

Chapter 3: No Child Left Behind: Highly Qualified Teachers and Paraprofessionals

To improve the quality of education we offer America's students, we need to put more well-qualified teachers in America's classrooms.

— Secretary of the U.S. Department of Education, Rod Paige, 2001

The quality and skill of a student's teacher is an extremely important factor in student achievement (Whitehurst, 2003). Congress recognized the importance of having well-prepared teachers in public school classrooms when they included provisions in the NCLB requiring that all new teachers hired in programs supported by Title I funds must be highly qualified teachers beginning with the 2002-2003 school year. Additionally, the law requires that by the end of the 2005-2006 school year, *all* teachers in public schools must be highly qualified. The NCLB also requires that states ensure that paraprofessionals who work in the nation's classrooms also are highly qualified. In this section we will review the NCLB's requirements regarding highly qualified teachers and paraprofessionals.

Highly Qualified Teachers

There are three basic requirements in the NCLB that public school teachers must meet to be highly qualified. First, teachers must hold a minimum of a bachelor's degree from a college or university. Second, teachers must have full state teacher certification or licensure for the area in which they teach. Third, teachers must be able to demonstrate subject matter competency in the core academic subjects in which they teach. Teachers can demonstrate subject matter competence by passing a state-administered test in each of the core subjects that he or she teaches. The structure and content of these tests are determined by the individual states.

To ensure that only highly qualified teachers teach in public school classrooms, each state that receives funds under Title I of NCLB must develop a plan to ensure that all of the state's public school teachers are highly qualified to teach core academic subjects in which they provide instruction. The NCLB regulations define core academic subjects as

45

English, reading-language arts, mathematics, science, foreign languages, civics, government, economics, art[1], history, and geography. If a teacher teaches in one of these core subjects, the NCLB highly qualified requirement applies to them. If a teacher teaches in more than two of these core subjects, he or she must be qualified in all the subject areas taught.

Who must be a highly qualified teacher?

Elementary School Teachers

Elementary school teachers must hold at least a bachelor's degree and be fully certified by the state in the area in which they teach. To demonstrate their knowledge and abilities they also must pass a test of subject matter knowledge. For elementary school teachers, this means passing a test of subject knowledge and teaching skill in reading-language arts, writing, mathematics, and other areas of the basic elementary school curriculum.

Middle and Secondary School Teachers

Both middle school and high school teachers must meet the same NLCB highly qualified standards. Both must have at least a bachelor's degree and be fully certified by the state in the area in which they teach. Because states may have different requirements for certification in middle school and certification in high school, teachers need to contact their state department of education to determine the appropriate certification requirements.

To demonstrate their knowledge and abilities they also must pass a state-administered test of subject matter knowledge. For the middle and high school teacher, this means passing a test in each academic subject in which he or she teaches. If a middle school or secondary school teacher provides instruction in more than one core academic subject, then he or she must be qualified in each area.

Special Education Teachers

Special education teachers must meet the same highly qualified standards as general education teachers. This means that they must (a) have a bachelor's degree, (b) be fully certified by the state in the area in which they teach, and (c) pass a test of subject matter knowledge.

---

[1] The NCLB includes "the arts" as a core academic subject, although it is up to the states to define what subjects constitute the arts.

Special education teachers in elementary schools must pass a state-administered test of subject knowledge and teaching skill in areas of the basic elementary school curriculum (e.g., reading-language arts, writing, mathematics). Middle and high school special education teachers who provide instruction in core academic subjects must meet the requirements of the law for being highly qualified in every core academic subject that they teach. This means they must test a state-administered test of content knowledge. This applies whether a special education teacher provides core academic instruction in a regular classroom, resource room, or another setting. For example, if a special education teacher provides reading instruction to students with learning disabilities, they have to be highly qualified in reading.

Special education teachers in middle schools and high schools often teach many subjects to their students (e.g., math, social studies, science). Rather than specializing in one subject area like most secondary teachers, however, special education teachers often specialize in working with students with certain disabilities covered by the Individuals with Disabilities Education Act (IDEA) (e.g., children with autism, learning disabilities, or emotional disabilities). Nonetheless, the NCLB requirements regarding being highly qualified in the core academic subjects they teach apply to them. Therefore, if special education teachers work with their students in core academic subjects, such as history, math, or science, they must be highly qualified in those subjects.

Many believe that this will place considerable burden on special education teachers, especially at the middle and high school levels, because it will require them to meet the highly qualified requirements in all the core academic subjects that they teach. Given the critical shortage of special education teachers and the diminishing number of teachers going into special education, these new requirements may prove to be a problem. The issue of what constitutes a highly qualified special education teacher under the NCLB may be revisited when the IDEA is reauthorized.

In IDEA reauthorization, Congress could address this issue and alter the highly qualified requirement for special education teachers. If Congress does not make any changes to this requirement in IDEA, then special education teachers will still have to meet the highly qualified requirement of NCLB.

There are activities, however, that special education teachers may take part in, that do not require them to be highly qualified. Such activities include providing consultation to highly qualified teachers of core academic subjects, using behavioral supports and interventions, selected appropriate academic accommodations, assisting students with study skills, and reinforcing instruction that a student has received in a core academic subject from a highly qualified teacher.

Teachers of Students with Limited English Proficiency

Similarly, teachers of students with LEP must meet the highly qualified requirements if they teach students in core academic subjects. Additionally, teachers of students with LEP must meet other ESEA requirements for teaching such as successful completion of an English proficiency test on oral, listening, and reading comprehension, and writing skills. If the teacher of students with LEP does not provide instruction in the core academic areas, they do not need to meet the highly qualified requirements; however, they still must meet the other ESEA requirements.

Teachers in Public Charter Schools

Teachers who teach in charter schools must hold at minimum a bachelor's degree and must demonstrate competence in the core academic areas in which they provide instruction. States, however, may determine whether a teacher in a charter school must be fully certified or licensed by the state. New teachers hired in Title I charter schools after the 2002-2003 school year must meet the highly qualified requirements. Teachers of core academic subjects hired to teach in charter schools before 2005-2006 must meet the highly qualified requirements.

What is a Charter School?

Charter schools are an alternative to traditional public schools. Although charter schools are publicly funded, they are free of many of the regulations that apply to public schools. This means that charter schools operate with greater autonomy than traditional public schools; nevertheless, they are still accountable to their sponsor. Charter schools must be nonsectarian in their programming and cannot charge tuition. Additionally, they must comply with federal nondiscrimination laws (e.g., Section 504) and the IDEA. Charter schools are usually created and managed by a group of parents, teachers, private managers, or community-based organizations.

The aims of charter schools vary widely, but typically they focus on providing increased opportunities for learning. Sometimes they include a focus on a specific set of educational objectives, an educational philosophy, specific teaching practices, or serving specific student populations. The specific operating procedures and goals are written into an agreement between the sponsoring agency and the school's organizers. This agreement is called a charter, and establishes the school's mission, goals, and ways to measure success. Charters are usually granted for 3 to 5 years and may be renewed when they expire.

Charter schools officially began in 1991 with the passage of the first charter school law in Minnesota. There are now more than 2,700 charter schools across the nation serving almost 700,000 students. Forty states and the District of Columbia have charter school laws.

Charter schools, because they are public schools, are subject to a state's AYP requirements including school improvement, school choice, supplemental education services, and corrective actions.

Who does not have to meet the highly qualified requirements?

Teachers do not need to meet the NCLB's highly qualified standards if they do not teach a core academic subject. Neither do the highly qualified standards apply to early childhood or pre-kindergarten teachers unless the state includes them in the state's definition of an elementary school. Short-term substitute teachers do not have to meet the highly qualified standards; however, the U.S. Department of Education suggests that long-term substitutes be highly qualified.

Special Situations

Current Teachers

The state must develop a system to ensure that teachers who are already teaching are highly qualified. Current teachers can demonstrate their competency and skills in the following ways. First, elementary teachers can demonstrate competency by passing a rigorous state academic subject matter test. Second, middle or secondary school teachers can demonstrate competency by having one of the following for each of the core subjects that they teach: (a) an academic major[2], (b) a graduate degree, (c) coursework equivalent to an academic major, or (d) an advanced certification or credential. Third, states can develop and use the high, objective, uniform, state standard of evaluation (HOUSSE).

If a teacher does not have one of these credentials, he or she either must pass a rigorous state test in each of the academic subjects in which he or she teaches or demonstrate competence based on the HOUSSE standards. States may develop a procedure by which current teachers can demonstrate competence in the subjects they teach by having their knowledge and ability evaluated based on criteria the state sets. The criteria must (a) be aligned with the state academic content standards, (b) be designed to provide objective information about the teacher's attainment of core content knowledge in the area in which he or she teaches, (c) be applied uniformly to all teachers in the state, and (d) take into consideration the time that the teacher has been teaching, although decisions cannot be based primarily on this consideration. This information must be made available to members of the public on request. If a state chooses to develop HOUSSE procedures, they must involve multiple measures of teacher competency and use rigorous and objective standards that all teachers are expected to meet or exceed.

---

[2] Having an academic minor does not make a teacher highly qualified in that area.

50

Alternative Certification

The NCLB gives states great flexibility when developing certification requirements needed to teach; however, the law also encourages states to have high standards for teacher certification. This includes certification through alternative routes. If teachers receive alternative certification, the state must ensure that the potential teacher (a) receives sustained high-quality professional development; (b) participates in a program that includes intensive supervision, structured guidance, and ongoing support or a teacher-mentoring program; (c) becomes a teacher for a period of time no more than 3 years; and (d) progresses toward full certification.

If teachers are teaching on an emergency or provisional license, they must take the necessary steps to become fully certified and meet the requirements of the NCLB. To become fully certified teachers must (a) get a graduate degree, (b) take coursework equivalent to an undergraduate minor, or (c) pass a state test in the academic subject in which he or she teaches.

FYI

What is Alternative Certification?

Alternative or nontraditional certification programs typically focus on training individuals to be teachers who did not choose teaching as their first occupation. For example, a mid-career professional or a person who just retired from the armed forces may be interested in becoming a teacher. Often, however, the traditional four years of undergraduate training may not be feasible. The goal of alternative certification programs is to provide a way for these individuals to prepare for a teaching career. The requirements for alternative certification vary by state.

Highly Qualified Paraprofessionals

Paraprofessionals play a valuable role in providing services to America's students. The NCLB allows paraprofessionals to provide instructional support services only when directly supervised by a teacher. Moreover, the teacher must plan all instructional activities and evaluate the achievement of the students who work with the paraprofessional.
The law clearly specifies what duties paraprofessional may perform. These duties include:

- Providing one-to-one tutoring (if scheduled when the student would not otherwise be taught by the teacher).

- Assisting with classroom management.

- Assisting in computer instruction.

- Conducting parental involvement activities.

- Providing instructional support in a library or media center.

- Acting as a translator.

- Providing instructional support services under the direct supervision of a qualified teacher.

For More Information

To find out more about working with paraprofessionals, go to the web site of the National Resource Center for Paraprofessionals at http://www.nrcpara.org/index.shtml

Another excellent resource is *Supervising Paraeducators in School Settings: A Team Approach* (ISBN 0-89079-713-7), edited by Anna Lou Pickett and Kent Gerlach. The book is published by Pro-Ed.

Qualifications of Paraprofessionals

Paraprofessionals who teach in Title I schools are covered under NCLB and must earn a secondary school diploma or a recognized equivalent. Additionally, paraprofessionals hired after January 8, 2002 must have completed 2 years of study at an institution of higher education or obtained an associate's degree or higher. Paraprofessionals without a degree can become highly qualified if they can pass a state or local test that demonstrates their knowledge of and ability to assist in teaching reading-language arts, writing, and mathematics or reading readiness, writing readiness, and mathematics readiness. For persons hired as paraprofessional prior to January 8, 2002, they must meet the NCLB standards by January 8, 2006.

The NCLB definition of paraprofessional does not include individuals who perform only non-instructional duties, such as clerical tasks, playground supervision, translating services, or providing personal care services. If the paraprofessional performs only these duties and does not facilitate instruction, he or she does not have to meet the NLCB's requirements.

Reporting Requirements

States must issue annual report cards on teacher qualifications. These reports must include (a) the professional qualification of teachers, (b) the percentage of teachers with emergency or provisional certifications, and (c) the percentage of classes in the state not taught by highly qualified teachers.

By the beginning of each school year, school districts that accept Title I funds must notify the parents of all students that they may receive information regarding the professional qualifications of their child's teacher. This notification and information must be provided in a uniform and understandable manner. If a parent exercises this prerogative, the school district must provide the following information about their child's teacher:

- If the teacher has met state qualification and state licensing criteria in his or her grade level or subject area;

- If the teacher is teaching under an emergency or provisional license;

- The major of the teacher in their college or university program, any other graduate degree he or she holds, and the field of the degree;

- If their child is receiving services from a paraprofessional and if he or she is receiving services, information about the paraprofessionals qualifications.

Title I schools must notify students' parents if a teacher of the core academic subjects who is not highly qualified has taught their child for 4 or more consecutive weeks. The law requires that this notification be completed in a "timely manner." Similarly, parents have the right to request information if their child receives services from a paraprofessional and the qualifications of the paraprofessionals.

Compliance with NCLB's Highly Qualified Teacher Requirements

States must submit plans to the U.S. Department of Education that (a) include measurable annual objectives, (b) show an annual increase in the percentage of teachers who are highly qualified, and (c) demonstrate that teachers in the state are receiving high-quality professional development. Additionally, these plans must ensure that all teachers of the core academic subjects achieve highly qualified status by the end of the 2005-2006 school year.

States must also delineate their plans to provide assistance to help public schools and school districts meet these requirements, and then to monitor schools' progress. In turn, all public school districts must develop their own plans regarding highly qualified teachers that include measurable annual goals and submit these plans to the state. Public school districts must also use at least 5% of their Title I funds to help teachers become highly qualified. Public school districts must meet their goals. If they do not meet their goals for 2 consecutive years, the state must provide the school district with technical assistance.

The school district, working with the state, will develop professional development activities that are grounded in scientifically-based strategies. Moreover, the state must ensure that the school district is using the research-based strategies.

Until all of a state's public school teachers are qualified, states are required to take steps to ensure that students from economically disadvantaged homes and students from racial and ethnic minorities are not taught at higher rates than other students by out-of-field, inexperienced, or unqualified teachers. Such steps may include transfers, professional development activities, and recruitment programs.

Professional Development

The NCLB requires states to provide high-quality professional development activities to all public school teachers. These activities must be grounded in scientifically-based research. Table 6 depicts professional development activities listed in NCLB.

Table 6: Professional Development Activities

Activities	Additional Information
• Improve and increase teachers' knowledge of the academic subjects the teacher teaches.	✓ Enables teachers to become highly qualified.
• Are integral parts of district-wide and school-wide educational improvement plans.	
• Give teachers, principals, and administrators the knowledge and skills to provide students with the opportunity to succeed at the state content standards.	
• Improve classroom management skills.	
• Are high quality, sustained, intensive, and classroom-focused to have a positive and lasting impact in classroom instruction and on teacher performance.	✓ Are *not* 1-day workshops or short-term workshops or conferences.
• Support the recruiting, hiring, and training of highly qualified teachers.	
• Advance teacher understanding of effective instructional strategies.	✓ These instructional strategies are: a) based on scientific research, and b) used to improve student achievement or substantially increase the knowledge and skills of teachers.
• Are aligned with and directly related to state academic content standards and assessments.	

- Are developed with participation of teachers, principals, parents, and administrators.

- Are designed to give teachers of students with limited English proficiency the knowledge and skills to provide appropriate instruction and support services.

- Are designed to provide training for teachers and principals in the use of technology and technology applications for the classroom.

- Are regularly evaluated for their impact on increasing teacher effectiveness and improving student achievement.

  ✓ The findings from the evaluations are used to improve the quality of professional development.

- Provide instruction in methods of teaching children with special needs.

- Provide instruction in the use of data and assessments to inform instructional practices.

- Provide instruction in ways that teachers, principals, and administrators can work more effectively with parents.

- Provide follow-up training to teachers who have participated in professional development activities to ensure that the knowledge and skills learned are implemented in the classroom.

Public school district personnel, teachers, and principals, working with the state department of education personnel, must develop these activities. These professional development activities must be grounded in scientifically-based research. This means that teachers must be taught research-based interventions and strategies that have a track record of improving student achievement. Moreover, states must ensure that the school districts are using scientifically-based professional development strategies.

States can assist public school districts to help adopt and implement more effective professional development activities by (a) developing guidelines for school districts on improving teacher quality, (b) providing technical assistance, (c) sponsoring conferences that address issues regarding professional development, and (d) disseminating information about research-based programs and practices. When developing a technical assistance program, states should consider the needs of special education teachers to become highly qualified and provide guidance to public school districts in coordinating resources for professional development.

Professional development activities may include forming partnerships with public school districts and institutions of higher education to establish school-based teacher training programs. These activities give prospective and beginning teachers an opportunity to work under the guidance of experienced teachers and college faculty. Similarly, states and school districts can create programs that enable paraprofessionals to obtain the education necessary to become certified and licensed teachers.

No Child Left Behind encourages states to adopt professional development opportunities that allow teachers to advance their careers without leaving the classroom. Such careers paths could include becoming (a) a career teacher, who stays in the classroom, (b) a mentor teacher, who stays in the classroom but receives additional pay for providing mentoring for new teachers, and (c) an exemplary teacher with a record of improving student achievement, who receives additional pay for training other teachers. The strategies are intended to help teachers advance their careers as teachers without leaving the classroom.

Funding Provided by No Child Left Behind

No Child Left Behind provides funds to states and public school districts to help them improve teacher quality through preservice and inservice training. Federal funding can be used to support a wide array of activities, including interventions for teacher professional development, when the activities are grounded in scientifically-based research. The law provides this funding in two major ways: first, NCLB gives states greater flexibility to target spending of their federal funds and second, Title II of the law provides grants to states and local school districts.

Flexibility in Using Federal Funds

Because of the increased flexibility available to school districts under NCLB, they can transfer up to 50% of the federal funds that they receive under different parts of the law (e.g., Title II–Improving teacher quality and enhancing educational technology, Title IV–Safe and Drug-Free Schools grants, and Title V–Innovative programs) to any of these programs or to their Title I program. The increased flexibility allows school districts to expend their funds as they decide without first seeking approval from the federal government to do so. Each district that receives Title I funds must spend at least 5% of their money on professional development to help their teachers become highly qualified.

Title II of No Child Left Behind

Title II of the NCLB is Preparing, Training, and Recruiting High Quality Teachers and Principals, and it provides grants to states and local school districts to increase student achievement by improving teacher and principal quality. The purpose of Title II grants is to assist states in increasing the number of highly qualified teachers in the nation's classrooms and highly qualified principals and assistant principals in the schools.

In their original NCLB accountability plans submitted to the U.S. Department of Education, states detailed their objectives for increasing the percentage of highly qualified teachers in the state's classrooms. Moreover, states had to describe how (a) they would use federal funds to meet the highly qualified teacher and paraprofessional requirements of the law, and (b) they would hold school districts accountable for assisting their teachers in meeting the highly qualified standard.

Title II provides funds for states to make subgrants to public school districts and state agencies of higher education for local projects to improve teacher quality. States may use these funds for administration and any of the following activities related to teacher and principal quality:

- Supporting professional development activities for principals and teachers;

- Reforming certification requirements for principals and teachers;

- Developing alternative routes to state certification;

- Assisting public school districts in recruiting and retaining highly qualified teachers and principals;

- Reforming tenure systems;

- Developing assessment systems to measure the effectiveness of professional development activities;

- Helping teachers meet certification and licensure requirements;

- Helping teachers use state standards and assessments to improve instruction and student achievement; and

- Training educators to integrate technology into their instruction.

Public school districts may apply for NCLB funds from the state. To apply, they must submit a plan that addresses a range of key issues, including a description of the professional development opportunities that they will make available to teachers and principals. School districts may use these funds for any of the following activities:

- Hiring highly qualified teachers;

- Providing professional development activities for teachers, principals, and paraprofessionals;

- Developing and implementing methods to recruit and retain highly qualified teachers, principals, and pupil services personnel;

- Reforming tenure systems;

- Providing merit pay;

- Testing teachers in their subject areas;

- Establishing innovative professional development programs, which may include partnerships with institutions of higher education;

- Providing professional development activities on improving classroom behavior;

- Developing teacher advancement plans to emphasize multiple career paths and pay differentiations, and

- Establishing programs for exemplary teachers.

The state must give priority to funding schools that (a) have the lowest percentage of highly qualified teachers, (b) have the highest average class size, or (c) have been identified as needing improvement.

School districts must conduct a needs assessment and detail the activities they will implement to increase the knowledge and skills that teachers need to improve student achievement, and to give principals the skills they need to provide meaningful assistance to teachers. Teachers must be involved in this process. States are required to monitor school districts to determine if they are making progress on their teacher quality goals. If a school district does not make progress on their goals for 2 consecutive years, the district must develop an improvement plan to address the reasons that they are not progressing. Additionally, when the school district is implementing the improvement plan, the state will assist the school district by providing technical assistance. If the school district fails to make progress after 3 consecutive years, the state must enter into agreement with the district regarding their use of Title II funds. This plan must include strategies to help the district meet their teacher quality objectives.

Additional Professional Development Grants Under NCLB

No Child Left Behind also contains several other grant programs targeted at improving teacher quality. These grant programs include the following:

- **Education Technology State Grants program.** The purpose of this grant program is to implement activities that improve student achievement through the use of educational technology. The program includes funding for high-quality professional development activities to assist teachers with integrating technology into their teaching.

- **Teaching American History.** The purpose of this grant program is to implement activities that promote the teaching of traditional American history in elementary and secondary schools as a separate academic subject and not as part of a social studies class. The program includes funds for professional development in teaching American history. To be eligible to receive a grant, school districts must partner with an institution of higher education, a nonprofit history or humanities organization, or a library or museum.

- **Civic Education.** The purpose of this grant program is to implement activities that improve the teaching of civics and government education, foster civic competence and responsibility, and improve civic and economic education in emerging democracies through cooperative exchange programs.

- **Math and Science Partnerships.** The purpose of this grant program is to provide professional development for mathematics and science teachers and to recruit mathematics, engineering, and science majors into teaching. Grants are available to partnerships that include an engineering, mathematics, or science department at an institution of higher education and a high-need school district.

- **Troops for Teachers.** The purpose of this grant is to assist eligible members of the military in being certified or licensed as highly qualified teachers. Additionally, the program assists school districts in hiring these teachers.

- **Transition to Teaching.** Grants are available to develop teacher corps or other programs to recruit and retain highly qualified mid-career professionals and recent graduates as teachers in high-need schools.

- **Early Childhood Educator Professional Development.** The purpose of this grant program is to enhance the school readiness of young children by improving the knowledge and skills of early childhood teachers who work in communities with high concentrations of poor children. Grants are available to partnerships that include at least one institution of higher education and one or more public agencies, such as Head Start.

- **School Leadership.** The purpose of this grant program is to support efforts to recruit, train, and retain principals and assistant principals to create a high-quality school leadership force. Because schools will now be held accountable for increasing student achievement and teacher quality, it is crucial that high-quality principals and assistant principals provide leadership in their schools. The program also provides funds for professional development activities for principals.

- **National Writing Project.** The purpose of this grant program is to train classroom teachers to teach writing effectively. The program authorizes federal grant money to the National Writing Project, a nonprofit educational organization. The organization contracts with institutions of higher education and nonprofit education advisors to operate programs and professional development activities to train teachers in scientifically-based writing instruction.

Summary of the Highly Qualified Teacher and Paraprofessional Requirements Under No Child Left Behind

No Child Left Behind requires that teachers in Title I schools be highly qualified before they can be hired. Additionally, NCLB requires that all teachers must be highly qualified by the end of the 2005-2006 school year. No Child Left Behind is very specific about the necessary knowledge and skills that a teacher must possess to be considered highly qualified. The law requires that teachers (a) be fully certified or licensed by the state in which they teach (emergency, temporary, or provisional licenses are not allowed), (b) hold a bachelor's degree, (c) demonstrate competency in knowledge and skills in teaching basic elementary school curriculum (elementary teachers) or in each of the core academic subjects that they teach (middle and high school teachers).

States are responsible for ensuring that all public school teachers in the state's classrooms become highly qualified by the target date. No Child Left Behind provides funds to states and school districts to assist them in meeting these goals by conducting a wide variety of professional development activities to improve teacher quality.

Important Dates

2002-2003 School Year

✓ New teachers hired with Title I funds must meet the highly qualified teacher requirements.

✓ New paraprofessionals hired with Title I funds must meet the highly qualified paraprofessional requirements.

2005-2006 School Year

✓ All teachers in core academic subjects must be highly qualified teachers.

✓ All paraprofessionals working in programs supported by Title I funds must be highly qualified paraprofessionals.

Discussion Questions

1. How does your state report to parents their children's teachers' qualifications?

2. What percentage of teachers in your state are "highly qualified" according to the criteria contained in NCLB?

3. How many teachers in your state are teaching under an emergency certification?

4. How will your state ensure that all teachers are "highly qualified" under NCLB by 2005-2006?

5. What forms of alternative certification are available in your state? How does your state ensure that alternative certification teachers meet the highly qualified standards of NCLB?

6. How does your state ensure that paraprofessionals are "highly qualified" under NCLB?

Chapter 4: Reading First

What is different about Reading First *is that for the first
time educational policy has been built on scientific
evidence. Typically, the federal government has given
states money for educational programs, but those
programs haven't been evaluated with respect to how well
they work. No longer can this country continue to support
practices that are not effective for all kids. We have to
close the gap between kids who are doing well and those
kids who are at risk for reading failure. For the first time,
we have a substantial converging body of evidence that
tells us what it takes for kids to learn to read, what
teachers need to know about how kids learn to read, why
quite a few kids have difficulty, and what you can do in
classroom and at home, from birth onward, to make sure
kids become good, proficient, and strong readers.*

— Dr. G. Reid Lyon, Chief, Child
Development and Behavior Branch, National
Institute of Child Health and Human Development,
National Institutes of Health, October 6, 2003

America's children are not doing well in reading. According to the
National Assessment of Educational Progress Report for 2002, 36%
of the nation's fourth-grade students score at a *below-basic* level.
Another 32% of our fourth graders only score at a *basic* level[3]. In other
words, less than 30% of America's fourth-grade public school students
read at or above a *proficient* level[4]. Furthermore, almost 70% of
economically-disadvantaged fourth-grade students and almost 50%
of fourth-grade students from urban areas read at a below-basic level.

Poor reading achievement is a critical problem for our children for
three primary reasons. First, reading is the fundamental skill upon which
all formal education depends, and if children can't read well, they likely
will fail in school (American Federation of Teachers, 1999). Second,
children who do not learn to read early in their school careers will almost

---

[3] The "basic" level in reading represents only partial mastery of the prerequisite
knowledge and skills that are essential for proficient reading (NCES, 2003).
[4] The "proficient" level in reading represents solid academic performance (NCES, 2003).

invariably continue to be poor readers (Torgeson, 2000). Third, poor readers tend to become less responsive to intervention as they grow older and their difficulties increase in scope and severity (Lane, Gresham, & O'Shaughnessy, 2002; Torgeson, 2000).

Fortunately, the research is clear that the vast majority of poor readers can be taught to read (Fletcher & Lyon, 1998). There is now a compelling body of empirical evidence about how literacy develops, why some children have difficulty learning to read, what teachers need to do to prevent reading problems, and what constitutes best instructional practice in reading (Lyon, 2003). Research findings show that the best solution to the problem of reading failure is to allocate resources for early identification and prevention (Torgeson, 2000; Vaughn & Schumm, 1996). In fact, longitudinal studies by the National Institutes of Health indicate that if educators can identify young children who are at risk for reading failure and then use *effective* instructional procedures to teach reading, the failure rate can be reduced to 5% to 6% even in the most disadvantaged areas (Lyon, 2003).

Research evidence clearly identifies the critical skills that young children need to learn if they are to become good readers (National Reading Panel, 2002). Moreover, teachers in reading programs throughout the nation have demonstrated that scientifically-based reading instruction does work with all children (National Reading Panel, 2002; U.S. Department of Education, 2002). A key to helping children become proficient readers early in their school careers is to inform every teacher about the components of research-based reading instruction and how to implement them. However, to ensure that these instructional practices are actually used in classrooms will require that teachers receive intensive competency-based inservice and preservice instruction in the science of teaching reading.

In NCLB, Congress and the President recognized that "teaching young children to read is the most critical educational priority facing this country" (U.S. Department of Education, 2002, p. 1). No Child Left Behind, therefore, includes an ambitious national initiative designed to help all children become successful readers by grade 3. The initiative is called Reading First. President Bush called Reading First the academic cornerstone of NCLB.

Reading First is designed to ensure that states and school districts receive assistance to (a) establish research-based reading programs for students in kindergarten through grade 3, and (b) improve teachers' skills in using these effective instructional practices. In this chapter, we examine Reading First, the largest early reading initiative this nation has ever undertaken.

Overview of Reading First

Reading First is authorized in Title I, Part B of NCLB. The program is the single most ambitious effort ever undertaken by the federal government to improve the reading skills of America's students. Three unique aspects of Reading First are that it (a) focuses on reading instruction that is supported by scientifically-based reading research, (b) provides a very large amount of money that states can receive in order provide training to teachers and to implement professional development activities, and (c) emphasizes early identification of children at risk for reading failure so that effective early instruction can be provided. The next section reviews the components of an effective reading program as detailed in the report of the National Reading Panel and the Reading First section of NCLB.

For More Information

For more information on Reading First, link to the U.S. Department of Education's guidance document in PDF or Microsoft Word at http://www.ed.gov/programs/readingfirst/legislation.html?exp=0

Components of Effective Reading Programs

Research clearly shows that learning to read early in life is fundamental to later school success. We also know that an alarming number of children fail to learn to read within the first years of schooling. Moreover, each year these children will most likely continue to fall further behind their average-achieving peers. Children who read poorly are a much greater risk of dropping out of school and encountering problems in post-school life than are children who read well.

Unfortunately, questions of how to teach reading in the first few years of schooling are a highly contentious and politicized topic. There is consensus, however, that improving the reading skills of the America's young children is a top priority of education. This priority is reflected in the NCLB's Reading First program.

To ensure that all children in America learn to read well by the end of third grade, Congress and the President emphasized the importance of using scientifically-based reading research. In other words, to teach reading successfully, Reading First requires that early reading instruction focus on instructional methods and strategies that have been proven to be effective for teaching young children to read.

FYI

What is scientifically-based reading research?

Scientifically-based reading research is research that applies the rigorous, systematic, and objective methods of science to obtain valid knowledge about the nature of (a) reading itself, (b) teaching reading, and (c) reading problems. Scientifically-based reading research includes research that:

- Relies on direct observational methods and objective measurements to provide valid data across evaluators and observers and across multiple measurements and observations;

- Controls, examines, or assesses factors directly related to reading;

- Involves rigorous data analysis to test the stated hypotheses and justify the general conclusions;

- Applies research that has been accepted by a peer-reviewed journal or approved by a panel of independent experts through a rigorous, objective, and scientific review.

In NCLB, Congress and the President relied on the conclusions of the National Reading Panel based on their review of over 100,000 scientifically-based reading studies.

What was the National Reading Panel?

In 1997, Congress directed the National Institute of Child Health and Human Development and the U.S. Department of Education to convene a national panel on reading. Fourteen reading experts, including leading reading researchers, representatives from higher education, teachers, administrators, and parents made up the National Reading Panel. The panel was charged with the task of assessing the status of scientifically-based reading research, including the effectiveness of various approaches to teaching children to read.

The National Reading Panel gathered information for their study in three ways. First, they reviewed public databases to determine what research had been conducted on how children learn to read. Second, the panel held public hearings to gather information about the public's needs. Third, the panel consulted with leading reading organizations.

The National Reading Panel located approximately 100,000 research studies on reading. In reviewing the research, the panel concentrated on alphabetics, phonemic awareness, phonics, fluency, comprehension, teacher preparation, teacher education and reading instruction, and computer technology and reading instruction.

The National Reading Panel concluded that for children to learn to read well, explicit and systematic instruction must be provided in five areas: phonemic awareness, phonics, vocabulary development, reading fluency, and reading comprehension strategies (National Reading Panel, 2002). These five components are listed and defined in Table 7.

Table 7: The Essential Components of Effective Reading Instruction as Listed in No Child Left Behind

Component	Definition	Findings
Phonemic Awareness	The ability to hear, identify, and manipulate the individual sounds, or phonemes, of spoken words.	Can be taught and it helps children to learn to read and spell. Children who enter school with little phonemic awareness experience less success in learning to read.
Phonics	The ability to understand and detect the predictable relationship between phonemes, the sounds of spoken language, and graphemes, the letters and spelling that represent those sounds in written language.	Phonics can be taught and is most effective when introduced early to children who are having difficulty learning to read. Systematic and explicit instruction in phonics is better than non-systematic or no instruction.
Vocabulary Development	The ability to store information about the meanings and pronunciations of words necessary for communication. The four types of vocabulary are (a) listening, (b) speaking, (c) reading, and (d) writing.	The four types of vocabulary can be taught. Children learn the meanings of many words through everyday experiences with language.

Reading Fluency	The ability to read text quickly and accurately.	Reading fluency and overall reading achievement can be improved by using repeated readings and monitored oral reading.
		There is no research evidence that instructional time spent on silent, independent reading improves reading fluency.
Reading Comprehension	The ability to read for understanding, to remember what has been read, and to communicate what has been read.	Reading comprehension can be improved by explicit instruction that assists the reader to use specific comprehension strategies.

Reading First specifically requires that states ensure that these five areas, which the law refers to as components of effective reading instruction, are included in their Reading First proposals. Similarly, when states determine which school district proposals to fund, the state must ensure that all programs, strategies, and activities that are proposed meet the criteria for scientifically-based reading research. The next section reviews the major features of Reading First.

For More Information

For more information on the National Reading Panel and its work, see the panel's web site at http://www.nationalreadingpanel.org/

See also the panel's report "Teaching Children to Read: An evidence-based assessment of the scientific research literature on reading and its implications for reading instruction" at http://www.nichd.nih.gov/publications/nrp/smallbook.htm

The publication can also be obtained by calling the National Institute of Child Health and Human Development at 1-800-370-2943 or ordering from the web site at http://www.nichd.nih.gov/publications/pubskey.cfm?from=nrp#National%20Reading%20Panel

The video "Teaching Children to Read" is also available from the site.

No Child Left Behind Grants to States

In 2002, the government authorized $900 million through the Reading First section of NCLB to be appropriated and provided to states in the form of 6-year reading grants. The grants were available to all states that wrote a successful proposal for Reading First funds. To be awarded funds, a state had to submit a proposal that passed a rigorous review process.

States submitting grant proposals have to provide detailed and comprehensive plans outlining their proposals to use research-proven methods and strategies to teach reading. States have multiple opportunities to write a proposal that satisfactorily addresses all the required Reading First program requirements. The U.S. Department of Education also provides technical assistance to help states develop their proposals according to the Reading First criteria. Therefore if states are unable to get funding, they are given help so that they can strengthen their proposals. The next section describes the Reading First grant proposal process.

The Reading First Leadership Team

The governor of the state and the head of the State Educational Agency (SEA) must establish a Reading Leadership Team prior to submitting their proposal for a Reading First grant. In addition to the governor and head of the SEA, the team should include:

- The chairman and ranking member of each committee in the legislature who are responsible for developing education policy.

- A representative from at least one local school district that is eligible to receive Reading First funds.

- A representative from a community-based organization that is involved in reading education.

- State directors of federal or state programs that have a strong reading component.

- A parent of a public or private school student or a parent who teaches his or her child at home.

- A teacher who successfully teaches reading (this may be a special education teacher).

- A family literacy service provider.

The reading leadership team may include additional participants, such as representatives from (a) institutions of higher education, (b) private nonprofit or for-profit agencies who base reading training on scientific evidence, and (c) school libraries or public libraries.

The task of the reading team is twofold. First, the team must monitor and examine the scientific base for reading instruction within the schools that need to improve reading achievement. Second, the team is to ensure that a seamless, complementary approach to reading achievement exists throughout the state.

State Proposals for NCLB Grants

When submitting a Reading First proposal, the state must describe its plan for implementing the Reading First program. The proposal must describe the state's plans to award competitive subgrants to public schools and to use leadership funds to improve reading instruction and student achievement. Additionally, all proposals must include the information listed in Table 8.

Table 8: Required Information in Grant Proposals

Components	Description
Reliable and Valid Assessment Plan	States must describe how they will assist local school districts to use screening, diagnostic, and classroom-based reading assessments.
National Evaluation Assurance	The applicant must agree that the SEA and local school districts will participate in the U.S. Department of Education's national evaluation of Reading First if the Department of Education requests the state to do so.
Scientifically-Based Reading Materials and Programs	States must describe how they will assist local school districts to identify instructional materials, programs, strategies, and approaches that are grounded in scientifically-based reading research.
Professional Development	States must describe how (a) professional development activities will be supported with Reading First funds, (b) these activities will improve instructional practices in reading, and (c) these activities will be grounded in scientifically-based reading research.
Essential Components of Reading Instruction	The state must describe how the funded activities will assist teachers to implement the essential components of reading instruction (i.e., phonemic awareness, phonics, vocabulary development, reading fluency, and reading comprehension strategies).

Subgrants to Local School Districts	States must describe how they will make competitive grants available to local school districts and how states will ensure that the school districts are using practices grounded in scientifically-based reading research.
Geographic Diversity	The state must describe how it will ensure that grant awards are available to school districts in both rural and urban school districts.
Program Coordination	The state must describe how it will build on and promote coordination among literacy programs in the state to increase their effectiveness in improving reading instruction.
Evaluation Strategies	The state must describe how it will assess and evaluate the effectiveness of the activities carried out under the program on a regular basis. Furthermore, states must use valid and reliable instruments to measure student progress and describe how it will use this data to determine if a school district will receive continued funding under Reading First.

After the grant proposal is submitted, it goes through a rigorous review process to determine if the state has demonstrated the capacity to improve reading achievement. As previously mentioned, the state may submit and re-submit their proposal until they successfully meet program requirements; the U.S. Department of Education will provide technical assistance to states to assist them in writing acceptable proposals.

When reviewing the state's plan, the expert review panel also expects to see that the state has described their plan for (a) using scientifically-based reading research to improve classroom reading instruction and its plan for achieving this goal, (b) providing leadership to approve and monitor the underlying scientific base of the instruction implemented in participating school districts and to effectively manage the state's Reading First program, (c) evaluating the effectiveness of its Reading First program and its method for reporting results annually, and (d) summarizing how the plan will result in improved classroom reading instruction and how a Reading First classroom will look.

For More Information

For more information on the expert panel's criteria for reviewing state proposals, see the Reading First PDF at http://www.ed.gov/offices/OESE/readingfirst/ReviewCriteriaFINAL.pdf

---

If a state submits a successful grant proposal, the federal government provides funds according to a poverty-based formula. The federal government distributes the funds according to the proportion of children ages 5 to 17 who reside within the state and from families with incomes below the poverty line compared to the number of all children in the state. Funds are provided for a 6-year period, contingent on sufficient appropriations and satisfactory state progress. The next section describes how states may use the federal Reading First money.

No Child Left Behind Funds Reserved for State Use

The U.S. Department of Education will award 6-year Reading First grants to states that submit successful proposals. States that receive these awards may use up to 20% of their total Reading First funding for such activities is (a) professional preservice and inservice development; (b) technical ssistance for local public schools and school districts; and (c) planning, dministering, and reporting grant activities. The purpose of these funds ; to assist states in building and maintaining a statewide capacity to teach ll children to read by the end of third grade. *All* Reading First funds used by states must be grounded in scientifically-based reading research as described in NCLB.

Professional Development

States may spend up to 65% of their 20% funding (i.e., 13% of a state's total Reading First funding) for professional preservice and inservice development for teachers from kindergarten though grade 3. The purpose of these professional development activities is to prepare teachers to teach reading by using scientifically-based instruction. Professional development activities may include providing teachers with information about instructional materials, programs, and approaches that are based on reading research. Moreover, professional development activities may target early intervention and the use of valid and reliable screening, diagnostic and classroom-based assessment instruments, and other procedures to identify children who may be at risk for reading failure or who are already having difficulty learning to read.

The professional development funds also can be spent on activities that strengthen and enhance preservice courses for students in public institutions of higher education preparing to teach children in kindergarten through grade 3. Activities can include reviewing course content to determine if it is consistent with current findings of scientifically-based reading research. If these activities are undertaken, the state must submit a report to the Reading Leadership Team and then make it available to the public through the Internet.

The state also may spend these funds to improve state licensure and certification standards. If the money is spent in this way, the Reading Leadership Team must make recommendations regarding how standards in the area of reading may be improved.

Technical Assistance

States may spend up to 25% of their 20% funding (i.e., 5% of a state's total Reading First funding) for technical assistance to local public schools and school districts. Technical assistance may involve aiding public school districts to design and implement a successful Reading First program. Such assistance may include (a) helping the school district to select and implement programs of reading instruction grounded in scientifically-based reading research; (b) selecting reliable and valid screening, diagnostic, and classroom-based reading assessments; and (c) identifying eligible professional development providers to prepare teachers to teach students by using reading programs grounded in scientifically-based reading research.

States may also spend their technical assistance funds to provide increased opportunities for students from kindergarten to grade 3 to receive assistance from alternative providers. Alternative providers must use programs and strategies that are grounded in scientifically-based reading research.

Planning, Administering, and Reporting

States may spend up to 10% of their 20% funding (i.e., 2% of a state's total Reading First funding) for Reading First planning, administering, and reporting activities. These activities include all planning related to the Reading First grants. Additionally, funds can be used to support administering the competitive subgrants to eligible school districts and using valid and reliable measures to assess and evaluate whether local school districts' Reading First activities have been effective in increasing the reading proficiency of children in grades 1 through 3. Funds can also be used to report activities to the U.S. Department of Education.

State Awards to Local School Districts

At least 80% of a state's total Reading First funds must go to local school districts[5]. States must award grants to school districts on a competitive basis; therefore, districts must apply for these subgrants. Additionally, the state must give priority to funding school districts that have at least 15% of their children from families with incomes below the poverty line or that have at least 6,500 children from families with incomes below the poverty line. These funds may be used only to serve students in kindergarten through grade 3. Figure 2 is a flowchart that depicts the flow of Reading First funds from the U.S. Department of Education to local school districts.

---

[5] Public charter schools that are local educational agencies under state law are eligible to apply for a Reading First grant if they meet eligibility criteria. Local school districts must also provide private school students and teachers in their jurisdiction Reading First funds on an equitable basis with public school children and teachers. In such situations, all services and benefits must be secular, neutral, and non-ideological.

Figure 2

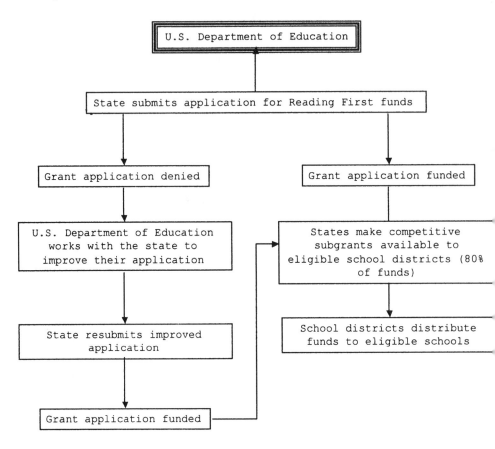

School districts that meet the following criteria are eligible to apply for Reading First funds. First, the school district must be among school districts in a state that has the highest percentages of students in kindergarten through grade 3 who are reading below grade level. Second, the school district's jurisdiction must include an empowerment zone or an enterprise zone[6], a significant number or percentage of schools that are identified under NCLB for school improvement, or high numbers or percentages of children who are from families in poverty and are counted for federal allocations under Title I. Local school districts or a consortium of school districts that meet these criteria may apply to the state for these Reading First subgrants.

The state should develop additional selection criteria that will distinguish among the quality of programs or approaches proposed by the applicants. Only those proposals that show real promise for successfully implementing effective research-based reading instruction and improving student achievement should be funded. States are responsible for ensuring that school districts use subgrant funds to implement high-quality programs that meet the requirements of Reading First.

Although states may designate the size of these subgrants, they must be sufficiently large enough funds to allow the school districts to make improvements in their reading instruction programs. Additionally, funds that are awarded to school districts cannot be used for planning activities but only for implementation activities.

School District Activities Required Under Reading First

School districts that receive a state subgrant under Reading First must carry out specific activities. The following section describes these activities.

Reading Assessment

School districts must select and administer reliable and valid screening, diagnostic, and classroom-based reading assessments. These assessments must measure student progress on the essential elements of reading instruction (i.e., phonemic awareness, phonics, vocabulary development, reading fluency, and reading comprehension strategies). Additionally,

---

[6] Empowerment and enterprise zones are high-poverty areas that receive special federal income tax treatment as incentives to encourage businesses to locate there.

these assessments must identify students who are at risk for reading failure or who have problems learning to read.

Reading Program

School districts must adopt and implement a program of reading instruction that is grounded in scientifically-based reading research and contains the five essential elements of reading instruction. Moreover, this instruction must be provided to children in kindergarten through grade 3 and children (a) with reading difficulties, (b) at risk for referral to special education for reading, (c) who were evaluated for services under the Individuals with Disabilities Education Act but who were not eligible for services, (d) who are in special education primarily due to a learning disability, (e) have deficits in the essential elements of reading, or (f) have limited English proficiency.

The program of reading instruction should have a design that includes explicit instructional strategies, appropriate instructional sequences, many opportunities to practice, and materials that are aligned to the instructional program. Moreover, the instructional program should also address a sufficient time allocated to reading instruction.

Instructional Materials

All instructional materials that the school uses must reflect scientifically-based reading instruction. These materials include any devices or services that are technological (e.g., software).

Professional Development

Schools must implement professional development activities for kindergarten through grade 3 teachers and kindergarten through grade 12 special education teachers. The purpose of professional development is to prepare these teachers to implement instructional programs that teach the five essential components of reading instruction. Furthermore, the professional development activities must prepare teachers to use screening, diagnostic, and classroom-based assessments to identify students who may be at risk of reading failure or have difficulty reading, and to monitor their progress in their reading programs. All professional development activities must be grounded in scientifically-based reading research.

Evaluation and Reporting Strategies

School districts that receive Reading First funds must collect and summarize data to document the effectiveness of their Reading First program in all schools that receive funds and in the school district. These data should be used to improve Reading First programs by identifying those schools that are producing significant gains in reading achievement. The school district must file a report to the state that details the data for all students and categories of students included in the adequate yearly progress (AYP) definition of NCLB.

Access to Reading Material

The school district must also promote and encourage reading and library programs that provide access to interesting and engaging reading materials.

Measuring Performance

The U.S. Department of Education requires states that receive Reading First funding to regularly evaluate the progress of the local school districts that are awarded subgrants. Moreover, states must use reliable and valid assessment instruments to measure student progress in reading achievement. The states should use these data to determine whether school districts should continue to receive Reading First subgrants. If, after assessing the data, the state finds that a local school district has improved reading achievement and implemented the program described in their proposal successfully and with fidelity, the state may award the district continuation funding. On the other hand, if a school district is not making progress in improving student reading achievement and implementing their program, the state may discontinue funding.

Whenever possible, states must contract with organizations that conduct scientifically-based reading research or program evaluations to evaluate their Reading First programs. The state must submit these evaluations to the U.S. Department of Education.

Each year states must submit reports on the state's implementation of their Reading First program to the U.S. Department of Education. Additionally, the state must submit a third-year report to the department that describes the reading achievement of students covered under the program. Table 9 describes the information that must be included in the state's annual reports.

Table 9: Information That Must Be in the Annual Report

Required Information	Description
Implementation Evidence	States must demonstrate that they are meeting the obligations of the Reading First program.
Achievement Gains	States must identify the schools and local school districts within the state that report the largest gains in reading achievement.
Program Effectiveness	States must report on the progress that school districts and the state is making in reducing the number of students reading below grade level in grades 1 to 3.
Reducing the Number of Students Who Are Reading Below Grade Level	States must report whether the state and local school districts have increased the number of students reading at or above grade level.

U.S. Department of Education Monitoring of States

The U.S. Department of Education will closely monitor states' implementation of the Reading First program and will hold them accountable for improving student reading achievement.

The Department will also contract with an independent external organization to coordinate and conduct a 5-year quantitative evaluation of the Reading First Program. The purpose of this scientifically-valid evaluation will be to assess the effects of the Reading First activities carried out by the states and local school districts. The results of the evaluation will be shared with the states and districts to assist them in program improvement. Table 10 describes the essential components of this evaluation.

Table 10: Evaluation of State Reading First Programs

Component	Description
1. Essential Components of Effective Reading Instruction	An analysis of the relationship between the essential components and overall reading proficiency.
2. Assessment Instruments	An analysis of whether the assessment instruments used by the states and districts measure the essential components of reading instruction.
3. State Reading Standards	An analysis of how the state reading standards correlate with the essential components of reading instruction.
4. Targeted Assistance Grants	An analysis of whether the receipt of targeted assistance grants results in an increase in the number of students who are proficient in reading.
5. Instructional Materials	A measurement of the extent to which specific instructional materials improve reading proficiency.
6. Identifying Reading Deficiencies	A measurement of the extent to which specific screening, diagnostic, and classroom-based instructional reading assessments assist teachers in identifying specific reading problems.
7. Professional Development	A measurement of the extent to which professional development programs implemented by states using Reading First funds improve reading instruction.

8. Preservice Preparation	A measurement of how well prepared preservice teachers entering the profession are to teach reading.
9. Student Interest in Reading	An analysis of changes in student's interest in reading and time spent in reading outside of school.
10. Additional Information	Any other pertinent information as determined by the U.S. Department of Education.
11. Reading First and Special Education	An analysis of the impact of Reading First on students' referral to and eligibility for special education because of reading problems.

Early Reading First

Early Reading First is a grant program in the NCLB that is funded at $75 million. It provides competitive grants to school districts and nonprofit organizations serving preschool children. The purpose of these grants is to support activities that improve children's pre-reading skills, especially children from low-income families. Funds must be used for screening, reading assessments, and any other appropriate programs grounded in scientifically-based reading research. Unlike Reading First, Early Reading First does not distribute funds to states, but rather distributes funds directly to schools.

The major goal of the Early Reading First program is to prepare children who enter kindergarten with the skills necessary for reading success. The programs that are funded under Early Reading First must be grounded in scientifically-based reading research. School districts or organizations that receive Early Reading First funds may use them for the following activities:

- Providing preschool children with high-quality oral language and language-rich environments.

- Providing scientifically-based professional development activities.

86

- Using effective and accurate screening assessments and progress monitoring instruments grounded in scientifically-based research to identify preschool-age children who may be at risk for reading failure.

- Identifying and providing activities and instructional materials grounded in scientifically-based reading research to support the development of oral language, phonological awareness, print awareness, and alphabet knowledge.

- Acquiring, providing training for, and implementing screening reading assessments and other appropriate measures to determine whether children are developing the early language and cognitive skills that they need for reading success.

- Integrating those instructional materials, activities, tools, and measures into the preschool program.

The NCLB also authorized federal money for independent evaluation of the effectiveness of the Early Reading First program. The purpose of the evaluation is to determine (a) how the grantees are improving the pre-reading skills of preschool children, and (b) the effectiveness of the professional development activities.

For More Information

For more information on Early Reading First, link to the U.S. Department of Education's guidance document available in PDF at http://www.ed.gov/offices/OESE/readingfirst/ReviewCriteriaFINAL.pdf

---

Summary

The goal of NCLB is to improve the academic achievement of our nation's students. The academic cornerstone of NCLB is the Reading First initiative. Reading First provides funds to help states and school districts implement effective instructional programs grounded in scientifically-based reading research. The initiative accomplishes this by providing grants to states whose proposals pass a rigorous review process. The states, in turn, award Reading First subgrants to local school districts to implement effective reading instruction and to provide professional development activities in effective reading instruction to teachers throughout the state.

Reading First is the first federal effort to focus on the scientifically-based critical elements of reading instruction: (a) phonemic awareness, (b) phonics, (c) vocabulary development, (d) fluency, and (e) reading comprehension. Schools and school districts must use Reading First funds to select instructional programs and materials and to implement professional development activities based on these critical elements.

Early Reading First is an effort to ensure that preschool children have the prerequisite skills needed to enter school ready to learn to read. This program provides funds to local school districts and public or private organizations that serve young children from low-income families.

Discussion Questions

1. How will your state help schools and school districts determine if their reading programs meet the standards of NCLB?

2. How does your state ensure that the principles of scientifically-based reading instruction are adopted in schools and school districts?

3. How does your state evaluate schools and school districts to ensure that they are improving reading achievement?

4. How does your state use the Reading First money that it retains and doesn't award to local school districts?

5. What professional development opportunities does your state offer educators to promote literacy development?

6. How does your state ensure that programs are in place to ensure that preschool programs meet the Early Reading First criteria of NCLB?

7. What professional development opportunities does your state offer early care and education providers to promote language and literacy development?

Chapter 5: Additional Provisions of No Child Left Behind

*After spending billions of (federal) dollars
on education programs, we have fallen short
in meeting our goals for educational
excellence. The academic achievement gap
between rich and poor, Anglo and minority
is not only wide, but in some cases is
growing wider still. In reacting to
...disappointing results, some have decided
that there should be no federal involvement
in education. Others suggest we merely add
new programs into a new system. Surely,
there must be another way – a way that
points to a more effective federal role.*

— President George W. Bush, Blueprint for
No Child Left Behind (p. 1)

NCLB is a massive and complex law. In previous chapters we have examined those components of the law that will have the most immediate effect on the states. There are, however, other significant components of this law that we have not yet presented. The purpose of many of these provisions is to offer federal money in the form of competitive grants to states. States often award much of this federal money to local school districts. The purpose of most of these grants is to award money to encourage states and school districts to adopt practices grounded in scientifically-based research or practices that seem promising based on initial research findings. In this chapter, we briefly explain additional important provisions of NCLB.

Unsafe Schools Choice Option

Purpose

The purpose of the Unsafe Schools Choice Option, which can be found in Title IX of the NCLB, is to allow parents, regardless of their income, to remove their children from a dangerous school setting. This option requires that states establish a policy to allow parents of children who are educated in unsafe schools to transfer to safe public schools.

Requirements

Each state, in consultation with a representative sample of local school districts, must determine what represents a persistently dangerous public elementary or secondary school. They must identify schools by using objective data such as the number of referrals to law enforcement, data on gang presence on school grounds, and results from student surveys on safety issues. When a school is identified as persistently dangerous, the state must (a) notify parents of each student in the school of the school's designation, (b) offer students the opportunity to transfer, and (c) transfer those students who exercise the choice option. Additionally the school district in which the persistently dangerous school is located must develop a corrective action plan and submit it to the state. The plan must be implemented in a timely manner. Moreover, the state should provide technical assistance and monitoring during the implementation of the plan.

There are two situations in which parents can exercise their option to move their child or children from an unsafe school. First, when a school is determined to be "persistently dangerous," the student must be allowed to transfer to a safe school. Second, when a student becomes a victim of a violent crime at school the student must also be allowed to transfer to a safe school. Each state's laws determine the types of offenses that the state considers violent criminal offenses. When a student has become the victim of a violent crime, the school district should offer the opportunity to transfer to a safe public school within 10 calendar days.

The state must allow students to transfer to a safe public elementary or secondary school, or public charter school, within the same district. To the extent possible, transfers that are allowed should be to schools that are making AYP and have not been identified as needing improvement or corrective action.

Compliance

To comply with this requirement of NCLB, each state must (a) develop an Unsafe School Choice Option policy, (b) identify persistently dangerous schools, (c) identify the types of offenses that are considered violent criminal offenses, (d) provide a safe public school choice option, and (e) certify compliance to the U.S. Department of Education. Moreover, NCLB funding is contingent upon states complying with this requirement of NCLB. The deadline for states to be in full compliance with the Unsafe Schools Choice Option was July 1, 2003.

Grants to States and School Districts

No Child Left Behind authorizes federal funds to states and school
districts, usually in the form of competitive grants. Although NCLB is
most often associated with standards, assessments, and accountability
mandates, the amount of federal funds that the U.S. Department of
Education will provide to states and school districts have the potential to
improve educational services to America's children and youth. Moreover,
these funds are contingent upon state and school districts developing and
implementing programs grounded in scientifically-based research. A list
of these grants and where they can be found in NCLB is provided in the
Appendix. The following sections briefly describe some of these
grant programs.

Safe and Drug-Free Schools and Communities

Purpose

Congress and the President believed that if schools are not safe and
orderly, teachers cannot teach and students cannot learn. Both teachers
and students need an environment that is safe, secure, and free of the
distractions of violence, drugs, and lack of discipline. A critical part of
NCLB, therefore, is the Safe and Drug-Free School and Communities
requirements. The purpose of the Safe and Drug-Free School and
Communities program is to (a) prevent violence in and around schools; (b)
prevent the illegal use of alcohol, drugs, and tobacco by children and
adolescents; and (c) foster a safe and drug-free learning environment that
supports academic achievement.

Requirements

The Safe and Drug-Free School and Communities program, which can be
found in Title IV, Part A of the NCLB, has two main components: a state
program and a national program. First, a state formula grant program

provides funding to the state's educational agency and the governor's office. The state, which receives 80% of the total funds, can award subgrants to school districts. The school districts may use these funds in turn for a wide range of drug and violence prevention activities. A portion of a state's federal fund under this program (i.e., 5%) can be used for state-level activities. These activities can include (a) technical assistance and training, (b) evaluation activities, and (c) program improvement services for school district and community groups.

The governor's office can receive up to 20% of the total funds. They can use these funds for awards to school districts and communities to provide services to children and youth with special needs, such as (a) youth who dropout of school, (b) students who are suspended or expelled, (c) children and youth who are homeless, and (d) students who are pregnant or parenting.

Second, the national program provides funding for model demonstration projects, special initiatives, technical assistance to states and school districts, evaluation activities, and other efforts to prevent drug abuse and violence. This program identifies who may apply for these funds and how they may be used. Table 11 lists and describes the grant programs that are included in the national program section of the Safe and Drug-Free School and Communities program.

Table 11: National Program Initiatives

Initiative	Description
Hate Crime Prevention	Makes grants available to school districts and community organizations to assist localities directly affected by hate crimes, by developing education and training programs to prevent hate-motivated crimes, and improving the conflict resolution skills of students and school staff.
Coordinator Program	Makes grants available to districts for hiring and training drug prevention and school safety coordinators in schools with significant drug and safety problems.
Community Service Grant Program	Makes grants available to states to implement programs for students who are suspended, expelled, or required to perform community service.
School Security Technology and Resource Center	Authorizes the U.S. Departments of Education, Energy, and Justice to establish resource centers that provide districts with technical assistance on school security, including security assessments for the use of technology, and to implement related research and data collection programs.
National Center on School and Youth Safety	Authorizes the U.S. Departments of Education and Justice to establish a center to implement activities related to school safety, including emergency response systems,

	anonymous student hotlines, consultation, information, and technical assistance. The center will give special attention to providing technical assistance to rural and impoverished communities.
Grants to Reduce Alcohol Abuse	Makes competitive grants available to districts to develop and implement programs to reduce alcohol abuse in secondary schools.
Mentoring Programs	Makes grants available to districts and community groups for mentoring programs for children who are at risk for educational failure, dropping out of school, involvement in criminal or delinquent activities, or who lack positive role models. The funds may be used to hire and train coordinators and recruit, screen, and train mentors, but they may not be used to compensate mentors.

Compliance

To receive federal funding under the Safe and Drug-Free School and Communities program, states must submit a comprehensive plan for how the state educational agency and the governor's office will use the Safe and Drug-Free School and Communities funds. In this document the state must include a state needs' assessment and develop state performance measures for all funded activities. These performance measures must be (a) derived from the needs assessment data, (b) focused on students' behaviors and attitudes, (c) consist of performance indicators with corresponding activities and levels of performance for each indicator, and (d) evaluated on a regular basis.

In the plan, the state must also ensure that (a) the governor's office will not duplicate state and school district prevention efforts, (b) they will cooperate with the U.S. Department of Education's evaluation and data collection activities, (c) they will use program funds to supplement, not replace or supplant, other prevention funding, (d) they will develop their plans in consultation with representatives of parent, student, and community-based organizations, and (e) they will establish a uniform management and reporting system for collecting information on school safety and youth drug use. Every 2 years, the state must file a report with the U.S. Department of Education that details the implementation, progress, and outcomes of their Safe and Drug-Free School and Communities program. Moreover, *all* state programs and activities must be grounded in scientifically-based prevention research.

For More Information

For more information on the Safe and Drug-Free School and Community Act link to the U.S. Department of Education's state grants guidance document available in PDF at http://www.ed.gov/programs/dvpformula/guidance.pdf

---

21st Century Learning Centers

Purpose

The purpose of the 21st Century Learning Centers program, which can be found in Title IV, Part B of the NCLB, is to help students, particularly students from low-performing schools, to meet state and local academic achievement standards. The program provides after school services to students and their families in academic enrichment, tutoring services, and other services designed to help students with academic achievement. Congress and the President believed that after school programs provide additional opportunities for closing the achievement gap between racial or ethnic groups, students from low-income environments and students from higher socioeconomic status, and male and female students. Furthermore, after school activities provide adult-supervised, constructive activities to keep older students constructively engaged who might otherwise participate in substance abuse and other undesirable activities.

Requirements

The 21st Century School program is a $1 billon state-administered grant program. In this program, state education agencies must submit a proposal for funding to the U.S. Department of Education. The proposal must include an explanation of how the state will award the funds to local school districts or other agencies that provide after school care and how they will provide training and technical assistance. Additionally, in the plan states must (a) describe how agencies receiving funding will be monitored and evaluated, (b) ensure that funded centers will be sustained after the funding ends, (c) ensure that the transportation needs of students who attend the after school programs will be addressed, and (d) involve appropriate state, local, and community officials and representatives of parents, teachers, students, and the business community in the process.

If the U.S. Department of Education funds the proposal, states request proposals for funding from agencies that provide after school services. Private or public agencies may apply for the funds. This includes school districts, community organizations, faith-based organizations, and government entities. States award the money to agencies with successful proposals. Funds may be used by the local agencies to improve students' academic achievement and other activities associated with youth development, including recreation and the arts.

Compliance

The 21st Century School program requires that the states follow four criteria to ensure compliance with the program. First, programs that are funded must be based on objective data regarding the need for after school activities, including summer school programs. Second, the state must have a set of performance indicators that are measurable and are directed toward ensuring quality programming. Third, programs must be grounded in scientifically-based research that provides evidence that the activities will help students meet state academic achievement standards. Fourth, states must plan and implement program planning and monitoring guidelines for local agencies that receive funding. States are required to report to the U.S. Department of Education on progress on meeting state standards for all local agencies that receive funds under the 21st Century Schools program.

Star Schools

Purpose

Nearly all of the nation's public schools and over 80% of the classrooms have access to the Internet. Additionally, distance learning is used in elementary schools and secondary schools across the country. Congress and the President believed that distance learning and the Internet could be used to provide high-quality instruction in remote or low-income locations where students do not have access to specialized courses.

The purpose of the Star Schools program, which can be found in Title V, Part D, Subpart 7 of the NCLB, is to improve instruction in academic subjects and vocational education by emphasizing learning opportunities for underserved populations through the use of telecommunications strategies, such as distance education.

Requirements

State agencies or multistate entities may write proposals for funding to the U.S. Department of Education. The proposals must provide instruction that is consistent with the state's academic content standards or provide assistance to states and school districts that are engaged in education reform activities.

Successful state proposals may be funded for periods of up to 5 years. If funded, the state must spend at least 25% of the funds for instructional programming and at least 50% for the cost of facilities, equipment, teacher training or retraining, technical assistance or programming for districts that are eligible for Title I grants. An additional 5% may be used for dissemination, evaluation, and other activities to enhance the quality of distance learning.

The Star School program also provides federal money for successful proposals to establish (a) statewide networks, (b) special local networks to demonstrate a high-technology programs to link elementary and secondary schools to institutions such as colleges and universities, and (c) continuing education programs that provide online access to educational services.

Compliance

Recipients of the Star School grants must demonstrate that they are providing effective services and using the grant funds appropriately. Additionally, to receive grant renewals, the recipients must show that they are continuing to provide services and will use grant funds to increase those services. Grant recipients must also agree to participate in program evaluations conducted by the U.S. Department of Education.

Parental Assistant Information Centers

Purpose

Congress and the President found that research clearly demonstrates that parental involvement in children's learning is positively related to academic achievement. Therefore, Congress included a section that provided funding for parent information centers. The Parental Assistance Information Centers program, which can be found in Title V, Part D, Subpart 16 of the NCLB, establishes school-based or school-linked parental information and resource centers that provide training, information, and support to parents and organizations that work with parents. The purpose of the centers is to support and implemental parental involvement strategies that lead to increased parental involvement and, thus, improved academic achievement.

Requirements

In the Parental Assistance Information Centers program, the U.S. Department of Education awards competitive grants to nonprofit organizations or associations of nonprofit organizations and school districts to establish the centers. Organizations that submit proposals must explain the types of training, information, and support they will provide.

Compliance

Each organization must submit annual information to the U.S. Department of Education on the effectiveness of the Parental Assistance Information Centers. The reports must contain information on the (a) number of parents who receive information and training; (b) nature of the training, information dissemination, and support activities that the center provides; (c) strategies used to serve parents who are limited English proficient, minority, or have limited literacy skills; (d) parental involvement policies and practices used by the center, and evaluation of whether these strategies are effective; and (e) effectiveness of the parental involvement activities of schools on improving student achievement.

Smaller Learning Communities

Purpose

Some research has indicated that students who attend smaller schools have higher rates of academic engagement, attendance, involvement, and achievement. Many believe that this is because smaller schools offer a personalized learning environment that more effectively engages their students.

The purpose of the Smaller Learning Communities program, found in Title V, Part D, Subpart 4 of the NCLB, is to provide support in efforts to create smaller learning environments by dividing large schools into smaller learning units. The program supports strategies to (a) restructure large schools by creating academies, houses, and schools-within-a-school, and (b) engage students by using teacher advisors, mentoring, and other innovations designed to personalize schools and to improve student achievement.

Requirements

The program provides competitive grants to school districts to create smaller learning communities within large schools. The grants may be used for funding a number of activities including the following: (a) studying the feasibility of creating smaller learning communities; (b) researching, developing, and implementing strategies for creating smaller learning communities; (c) providing professional development for school staff in innovative teaching methods that can be used in smaller learning communities; and (d) developing and implementing strategies that increase parental, business, and community involvement in the smaller learning communities, thereby providing links between students, their parents, and the community, and increased professional development opportunities for teachers.

Compliance

When developing a proposal for funding, school districts must describe the (a) strategies and methods they will use to create smaller learning communities, (b) curricula and instructional practices that would be used in the smaller learning environment, (c) processes for involving parents, teachers, and other interested parties in developing smaller learning communities, and (d) methods for placing students in smaller learning communities. School districts that are awarded the grants must ensure that they implement these strategies and must measure their progress by tracking changes in students' test scores, attendance and graduation rates, and courses that students take.

Public Charter Schools

Purpose

In 1991 charter schools began in Minnesota as an alternative to traditional public schools. Although charter schools are publicly funded, they are free of many of the regulations that apply to public schools. However, they must adhere to the basic requirements set forth by the state in which they are located. They are autonomous, alternative public schools often run by parents, teachers, community members, and for-profit companies. Their purpose was to offer increased local control of education, thereby increasing options within the public school system. Charter schools often offer unique educational practices and sometimes specialize in a particular area (e.g., back to the basics, technology). Some charter schools are specifically designed to serve gifted and talented students or students at risk for school failure.

No Child Left Behind includes charter schools as a choice that must be offered to parents when a school is designated as needing improvement, corrective action, or is in restructuring. Additionally, NCLB includes a competitive grant program that provides financial assistance to both states and individual charter schools. The Public Charter Schools program can be found in Title V, Part B, Subpart 1 of the NCLB.

Requirements

States with charter school laws may submit proposals to the U.S. Department of Education for grants. If a state doesn't submit a proposal for a grant or if their proposal is denied, individual charter schools in the state may submit proposals for funding. The proposal must explain how the state will (a) establish procedures and guidelines for administering a competitive subgrant program, (b) determine who is eligible for the subgrants and the proposal guidelines they must follow, and (c) develop

101

and implement program planning and monitoring guidelines for agencies that receive grants.

Grant funds may be used for planning, developing, and implementing charter schools. Additionally, grant funds can be used to disseminate information about a charter school or schools.

Compliance

States and school districts that receive funding through the Public Charter Schools program must demonstrate the contribution that the charter schools make in assisting educationally disadvantaged and other students in meeting the state's academic standards. Moreover states must hold charter schools accountable for meeting clear and measurable objectives for the academic achievement of their students.

Magnet Schools Assistance

Purpose

Magnet schools are public schools that offer innovative programs in specific areas (e.g., computers, science, arts, communications). They are often very competitive and selective schools that are known for their special programs. Magnet schools are designed to attract a diverse group of students based on their interests or abilities. Magnet schools were developed in the 1970s to help desegregate public school systems by encouraging students to attend schools that were not in their neighborhoods. In fact, student diversity is often an overt goal of magnet schools.

The Magnet Schools Assistance program, which can be found in Title V, Part C of the NCLB, is a competitive grant program that provides federal funds to school districts or consortiums of school districts to establish and operate magnet schools in school districts that are under court-ordered or federally-approved voluntary desegregation plans. The intent of the magnet school program is to reduce, eliminate, or prevent minority group isolation in public elementary and secondary schools.

The purpose of the program is to build a grantee's capacity to create and operate magnet schools. Funding priority is given to applicants who demonstrate the greatest need for assistance.

Requirements

School districts write proposals for funding and submit them to the U.S. Department of Education. These proposals must explain how the district or districts will (a) develop and implement magnet school programs, and (b) select students for the magnet school by methods such as a lottery, instead of using academic achievement. Grant funds may be used to employ teachers and acquire books, equipment, and other materials and for professional development activities.

Compliance

Districts that are funded must use the funding to eliminate minority group isolation and increase academic achievement. Additionally, grant recipients must continue the magnet schools after the federal funding is discontinued. Furthermore, recipients must follow NCLB specifications such as (a) employing highly qualified teachers, and (b) encouraging greater parental involvement. Grant recipients must also participate in federal evaluations if requested to do so.

Enhancing Education Through Technology

Purpose

Research supports using technology to enhance curricula and to engage students in learning. Moreover, advancements in technology are reflected by the current job market, which often demands technology skills in the workers. Unfortunately, research also reveals a divide between the amount of technology available to students in high-poverty schools and in low poverty schools. Another problem with classroom-based technology is that often teachers are unprepared to use it effectively in their teaching.

The Enhancing Education Through Technology program, which can be found at Title II, Part D, Subparts 1 and 2 of the NCLB, awards federal grants to states. States may use 5% of the total award for state-level activities. Fifty percent of the remaining funds must be distributed to school districts based on the level of poverty and the other 50% to high-need school districts[7] on a competitive basis.

Furthermore, the funds can also be used nationally for three purposes. First, the federal funds may be used to support national

---

[7] High-need schools districts are those districts that are high poverty and have at least one low-performing school or have a great need for technology.

dissemination of information on best practices in using technology in the classroom. Second, funds can be used to provide technical assistance to states and school districts. Finally, funds can be used for rigorous long-term studies of the educational technology practices and strategies that will improve teaching and learning.

The major purposes of NCLB's Enhancing Education Through Technology program are to (a) improve student academic achievement through the use of technology in elementary and secondary classrooms, (b) assist all students to become technology literate by the end of eighth grade, and (c) encourage the effective integration of technology devices and systems with teacher training and high-quality professional development to establish research-based instructional programs and models. The program emphasizes funding technology development in school districts that serve many children from low-income families.

Requirements

States must have technology plans that include state goals for (a) using technology, (b) preparing teachers to use technology, (c) providing technical assistance to high-poverty districts, and (d) ensuring that appropriate accountability measures are used to evaluate the effectiveness of the Educational Technology State Grants program. States and school districts may use funds to develop progress monitoring systems.

Districts that receive funding under this program must spend 25% of their funds on high-quality professional development activities. States may exempt school districts from this requirement, however, if they demonstrate that they already provide high-quality professional development in the use of technology.

Compliance

This program focuses on using technology to improve curricula, instruction, and achievement by ensuring that school districts have the resources needed to integrate technology into the classroom. Districts that participate in this program must develop accountability measures to assess how effective they are at (a) integrating technology into the curricula, (b) increasing the ability of teachers to teach with technology, and (c) enable students to meet the challenging state academic content standards. Additionally, the U.S. Department of Education will conduct a study to identify the conditions under which technology increases student achievement and teachers' ability to teach using technology improves.

Dropout Prevention

Purpose

According to the National Center for Education Statistics (2003), the national dropout rate has been close to 11% over the past decade. Moreover, many groups of students (e.g., students from families with low incomes, African American students) have even higher dropout rates. No Child Left Behind assists schools with dropout rates above their state averages to implement effective dropout prevention programs and school reentry through the School Dropout Prevention program. This program can be found in Title I, Part H of NCLB.

The School Dropout Prevention program is a grant program for states and school districts to help them implement coordinated and sustainable school dropout prevention and school reentry programs that are grounded in scientifically-based research. The program also includes a national recognition program to identify schools that are implementing comprehensive efforts that have been successful in lowering school dropout rates for all students. The U.S. Department of Education will also establish a national clearinghouse on information regarding effective school dropout prevention and school reentry programs and an interagency group to determine how federal programs can help reduce school dropout rates.

Requirements

The School Dropout Prevention program authorizes competitive grants to states. The states make subgrants available to local school districts. For school districts to be eligible for subgrants, the district must operate at least one school that (a) serves students in grades 6 through 12, (b) receives funds under Title I, and (c) serves a student population of at least 50% from low-income households.

Proposals for School Dropout Prevention funds must identify those schools with dropout rates above the state average and describe the strategies to prevent school dropout and facilitate student reentry into school. Moreover, these strategies must conform to scientifically-based research in dropout prevention and reentry.

School districts that receive funds may spend the federal dollars on implementing professional development programs, reducing student-teacher ratios, developing counseling and mentoring programs for at-risk students, implementing comprehensive school reform models, and other research-based strategies. Additionally, the school district must provide technical assistance to any secondary schools receiving program funds that have not made progress in lowering their dropout rates. The U.S. Department of Education will also provide technical assistance to states and school districts to help them develop and implement effective school dropout prevention programs.

Compliance

The U.S. Department of Education is responsible for evaluating the effectiveness of school dropout prevention efforts funded under this program by collecting data on the effectiveness of funded programs. States that receive dropout prevention programs must file annual reports to the U.S. Department of Education on the implementation of program activities and outcome data for students in schools that receive program funds. The outcome data must include dropout rates disaggregated by race and ethnicity for 2 years prior to receiving the funds and during each year of funding.

Arts in Education

Purpose

The Arts in Education program, which can be found in Title V, Part D, Subpart 15 of NCLB, supports education reform by strengthening arts education programs. The purpose of the program is to help all students meet challenging state academic content standards and achievement standards in the arts.

Requirements

The U.S. Department of Education will provide funding to states, school districts, institutions of higher education, museums or other cultural institutions, and other public or private organizations. Funds may be provided through competitive grants or contracts. The art education funds may be used for activities such as (a) researching art education, (b) disseminating models of best practices, (c) developing state arts education assessment based on a state's content standards, or (d) developing curriculum frameworks. Additionally, the funds must be used to supplement, not replace, existing funds.

Compliance

Grantees should coordinate their efforts with public or private cultural agencies or cultural organizations such as museums, arts education associations, libraries, and theaters. Grantees must agree to participate in evaluation activities that are conducted by states or the U.S. Department of Education.

Summary

No Child Left Behind is usually associated with the accountability requirements and adequate yearly progress. There are, however, many other important aspects to NCLB. One of these components is the Unsafe Schools Choice Option, which allows parents to remove their child to a safe school when he or she has been the victim of a violent crime on school grounds or is being educated in a persistently dangerous school.

Another extremely important aspect of NCLB is the large amount of federal funds that it will award to states and school districts in the form of grants. In these grants the U.S. Department of Education provides federal money to states. The states, in turn, award much of this federal money to local school districts. The purpose of most of these grants is to encourage states and school districts to adopt practices grounded in scientifically-based research or practices that seem promising based on initial research findings. Additionally, accountability systems are built into these grants to ensure that the grant funds are spent appropriately and that the programs that are implemented using these funds lead to measurable and positive results. The unprecedented large amount of federal funding that is available to states and local school districts has the potential to have a significant impact on schools and school districts throughout America.

Discussion Questions

1. Are there any "persistently dangerous" schools in your state? If so, what actions are be taking to improve safety in the school(s)?

2. For which grant programs has your state applied?

3. Has your state enacted a charter school law? If so, will it participate in the federal charter schools program?

4. Has your state has applied for Safe and Drug-Free School and Communities money? If so, how will it use the money? What school districts in your state have received Safe and Drug-Free School money? How are they using the funds?

5. If your state participates in the grant programs, how does it choose school districts to receive subgrants?

6. How does your state monitor the effectiveness of programming in school districts that receive grant funds?

Chapter 6: The No Child Left Behind Act of 2001: Implications for Administrators, Teachers, and Teacher Trainers

*I have a vision of a day in which every child
receives an education that is good enough, a
day in which no child's future is crippled by
a bad teacher or a bad curriculum or a bad
school, a day in which we figure out how to
deliver an effective education to
everyone...When that day comes, it will be
because the nation has learned to ground
educational practice in science, and when
the education research community has
learned to engage in a science that serves.*

— Grover (Russ) Whitehurst, Director
of the Institute of Education Sciences
in the U.S. Department of Education,
September 24, 2003

No Child Left Behind is a comprehensive and complex law that increased federal education funding to unprecedented levels. The law also represents the most significant expansion of the federal government into education in history. No Child Left Behind increases federal mandates and requirements for states, school districts, and public schools.

The law represents a logical step in a series of education laws passed by the federal government that were intended to improve the academic achievement of the nation's students. Since the mid-1960s, the federal government has provided very large amounts of money to states to assist them in improving educational programming for public school students. Beginning with *A Nation at Risk* (1983), officials in the federal government began to question the results that federal funding was having on the state's educational systems. Many believed that the evidence reported in *A Nation at Risk* clearly showed that the federal funds were not being spent on meaningful state activities designed to improve educational results. Moreover, legislators argued that the federal funds should be spent in a more effective manner.

The federal role in education began to expand in The Improving America's Schools Act of 1994, America 2000, and Goals 2000. These laws created a new role for the federal government in public and secondary education by tying government funding to the development of rigorous academic content standards by the states. Unfortunately, although states began to develop these standards, increases in student achievement were not occurring. No Child Left Behind's unique contribution was to expand the role of the federal government in public education by holding states, school districts, and schools accountable for producing measurable gains in students' academic achievement. For the first time, the federal government required states and school districts to use numerical data that provides evidence of improved student outcomes.

In this edition of the Merrill/Prentice Hall Student Enrichment Series, we have examined the NCLB Act of 2001 and its purpose, goals, and major provisions. This massive law consists of multiple components. Some of these components will directly affect district administrators, principals, and teachers. In the next section we discuss the implications of the NCLB for school districts and school personnel. We emphasize what personnel need to know to meet their responsibilities under the law.

Implication #1: Know the Law

Because of the strict accountability requirements of NCLB, it is vital that administrators know exactly what the law requires of them. The consequences of failing to meet the requirements of NCLB are serious. Failing to meet these requirements because of a lack of knowledge is inexcusable. Consider the following scenario. A school principal is not aware of that 95% of all of his or her school's students, including students in the specific subgroups, need to be tested during statewide achievement testing, and as a result fails to meet the NCLB's accountability criteria. His or her school does not make AYP because of the error. Because of this error, the school could be targeted for corrective action or restructuring. Similarly, if teachers are unaware that they need to be certified in a specific area and miss the state certification test or fail to take a course needed for certification, the error could cost them their job.

Adhering to the requirements of the NCLB can be a daunting task; nevertheless, school districts must ensure that all district administrators, teachers, and staff are well-trained in their responsibilities under the law. Moreover, preservice teachers need intensive training to prepare them to enter schools knowing what is required of them and their schools under NCLB. The next section briefly discusses implications for school district personnel and teacher trainers.

School District Administrators

Every public school district should have at least one district level administrator who specializes in the NCLB. This person should be charged with two major areas of responsibility. First, he or she must ensure that the school district, and every school in the district, is in compliance with NCLB (e.g., hires highly qualified teachers, ensures that the proper number of students in each subgroup are being tested on the statewide assessment systems, disaggregates testing data by subgroup, includes required information on district report cards). Second, he or she must ensure that the school district, and every school in the district, meets the requirements of the law in schools that are targeted as needing improvement, corrective action, or restructuring (e.g., develops and implements a school improvement plan, offers public school choice, uses eligible supplemental educational service providers, assists parents to choose a provider from a state approved list). Moreover, this person must ensure that all school district administrators, principals, and teachers are well-trained in their responsibilities under NCLB.

School Principals

Because principals are ultimately accountable for everything that occurs in their schools, they must be aware of their responsibilities, as well as their teachers' responsibilities, under NCLB. This includes ensuring that parents of the school's students receive notices when required under NCLB (e.g., school choice, supplemental service providers), that all teachers and paraprofessionals meet the NCLB's requirements for highly qualified teachers and paraprofessionals, and that the required numbers of students in the various subgroups are tested on the statewide assessments.

Teachers

There are many NCLB requirements that directly affect teachers. They must know their responsibilities and act accordingly to meet them. Especially important to teachers are the NCLB's requirements regarding (a) teacher certification and qualifications and certification; (b) statewide testing requirements for all students, including students in the specified subgroups; and (c) the appropriate duties of paraprofessionals.

Teacher Trainers

Teacher-training faculty in colleges of education must thoroughly prepare preservice teachers in NCLB. New teachers should understand the

111

purpose and major principles of the law and know and be able to implement the requirements of the law that specifically pertain to them (e.g., state certification standards and the highly qualified requirements; statewide testing requirements for all students, including students in the specified subgroups; the appropriate duties of paraprofessionals). Teacher-training institutions that do not prepare their prospective teachers to carry out their responsibilities do a disservice to these preservice teachers, the schools in which they will work, and the students that they will teach.

Implication #2: Assess Students for Instruction

When a student fails to learn it is often because the student's abilities and the instructional program do not match. When this happens, teachers need to make good decisions about instructional programs and procedures and revise them effectively. To make good decisions regarding student learning, it is imperative that teachers have good information. This is only possible when teachers understand how to do an effective assessment. When teachers can construct and administer appropriate and relevant assessments it increases the likelihood that students with reading and math problems can be identified and provided with interventions conforming to scientifically-based research that match their learning needs. If this can be done, teaching will be more effective, thus raising students' academic achievement levels.

It is also critical that school districts, schools, and teachers use assessment systems that will enable teachers to identify students who are experiencing reading and math problems so that they can be targeted for interventions that can prevent these problems from becoming more serious. If teachers can determine what students know and don't know, they can appropriately match the student's abilities with the instructional program. The key issue in prevention is identifying students with problems early enough so teachers can intervene effectively and thus remediate before they experience academic failure.

A mistake that educators often make is assuming that standardized norm-referenced tests are the only types of assessments that give teachers valuable information. Such tests are useful for determining general achievement levels, but are not sensitive enough to make appropriate instructional decisions. For these purposes, curriculum-based assessments and criterion-referenced assessments are more appropriate. The next

112

section briefly discusses implications for school district personnel and teacher trainers.

School District Administrators

School districts should have personnel with expertise in implementing the statewide assessment system. Additionally, they should have expertise in developing and conducting appropriate and relevant assessments that lead to meaningful instructional programming. The people in this position should be responsible for ensuring that the (a) appropriate numbers of students in all disaggregated subgroups are administered the statewide examination, (b) results are disaggregated and reported to the appropriate personnel in the state department of education, and (c) information is reported to parents in the district report card. The district assessment personnel should also assume responsibility for appropriate teacher inservice development activities for assessment procedures.

School Principals

The primary role of the principal for student assessment is to ensure that teachers are knowledgeable about their assessment responsibilities and that they carry them out in an appropriate manner. Principals should monitor student achievement and work with teachers who are having difficulties. Additionally, they should arrange appropriate professional development activities.

Teachers

For teachers to be successful in improving the achievement levels of their students, especially students with academic difficulties, they must have expertise in (a) constructing and implementing relevant assessments, (b) gathering information using these assessments, (c) interpreting these assessments, and (d) matching instruction programs and strategies to the assessment results. Good teaching requires good information, and good information is collected through the assessment process. Teachers should take advantage of professional development activities that help them become more efficient and effective in assessing the instructional needs of the students whom they teach.

Teacher Trainers

Teacher-training faculty in colleges of education must thoroughly prepare preservice teachers to (a) develop assessment instruments, (b) interpret assessment results, and (c) base instructional decisions on the assessments.

No Child Left Behind focuses on increasing student achievement. If students have difficulties learning in the regular curriculum, teachers must be able to assess their educational needs and respond to them with meaningful instruction. Teacher-training programs must offer their preservice teachers opportunities to learn and practice constructing and interpreting relevant assessments.

Implication #3: Use Instructional Procedures Grounded in Scientifically-Based Research

One of the central principles of NCLB is that federal funds will support only educational procedures, materials, and strategies backed by scientifically-based research. This principle of NCLB requires that teachers use procedures and strategies endorsed by scientifically-based research findings and thus offers a great opportunity to bring evidence-based practices to America's elementary and secondary classrooms.

There is a huge gap between (a) what educators and researchers know works from scientifically-based research, and (b) what is actually taught in many teacher-preparation programs and then done in classrooms. Unfortunately, no other profession has as much acrimonious dispute regarding what constitutes effective practice as does education. Usually, both sides in a debate will cite supposed studies or research that support their positions, although often this research will be based on ideology, values, hunches, or tradition rather than scientifically-based research. Carnine (2000) asserts that in other professions, such as medicine and engineering, research is taken seriously because it brings clarity and progress to the professions. However, Carnine believes that educators often ignore the findings of research because it does not fit with their ideological preferences. NCLB is moving education away from philosophy and toward science.

No Child Left Behind focuses on embracing teaching methods and procedures that scientifically-based research supports as increasing student achievement. According to the writers of NCLB, the knowledge base of scientifically-based research practices in reading, math, and other academic subjects must be the core of our educational practices if we are to affect meaningful changes in our schools. The next section briefly discusses implications for school district personnel and teacher trainers.

School District Administrators

Educational research seldom makes its way into the classroom. Education tends to lurch from one fad to another with little regard for rigorous evidence. Until education becomes a profession that understands and uses evidence from research, the use of unproven and faddish practices will continue and, unfortunately, will be reflected in lowered student achievement.

Most school districts have administrators responsible for staff development activities. Moreover, state departments of education have people with expertise in particular areas that are in positions to influence educational practices in schools. No Child Left Behind puts educators under intense pressure to produce better results. School district personnel are well-positioned to ensure that research-based practices are used to educate students.

To meet the requirements of NCLB school districts must abandon practices based on sales pitches, traditions, fads, or ideological preferences and embrace scientifically-based research evidence. School districts may want to consider forming review panels that are collaborative efforts that include district administrators, principals, and teachers to assess the research base in adopting curriculum or instructional procedures. Only when school districts adopt proven methods will they be able to meet the accountability requirements of NCLB.

School Principals

School principals are the instructional leaders in their schools. Thus, they also have the standing to ensure that their teachers use evidence-based instructional materials and procedures. To properly fulfill their roles, principals must be able to distinguish between scientifically-based instructional practices and unproven methods to ensure that evidence-based methods and procedures are being used in their schools. This will require that principals be able to access and judge information as either proven or unproven based on science, and not on opinion. Principals are ultimately responsible for ensuring that students in their schools make academic progress; when teachers use research-based methods in their teaching, as required by NCLB, real academic progress will be the likely result.

Teachers

The role of scientifically-based research on instructional practices will not impact students' academic achievement unless such practices are actually used in classrooms. Unfortunately, teachers may be put in positions in which they are forced to adopt unproven practices by well-intentioned, but ill-informed, school district officials or principals. Moreover, their teacher-training programs may rely more on ideology than science. In such situations, the only way that a teacher can determine which educational practices are research-based and which teacher training programs and professional development activities will prepare them to use research-based methods is to become an educated consumer who is able to distinguish between fad, ideology, and science.

Teacher Trainers

Teacher-training faculty members in colleges of education must thoroughly prepare preservice teachers to use scientifically-based and researched instructional practices and to become themselves educated consumers of research. To do this, faculty members must become connected to the empirical bases in their fields and prepare their students to discriminate between proven and unproven educational methods and strategies, and testimonial and empirical evidence.

Collecting Meaningful Data on Student Progress

Teachers need to collect meaningful data on their students' progress, especially in reading and mathematics, to ensure that their programs are working. Additionally, these data should be collected during the course of instruction, so that the teacher's instructional decisions are guided by what the student is currently doing or not doing. The purpose of collecting data is to provide objective evidence of a program's effectiveness and to guide instructional decisions. Teachers can ensure that they provide meaningful instruction by collecting useful data on a student's progress and then by using the data to inform their instructional decisions. In other words, teachers can adjust their instruction in response to student performance. Collecting data during the course of instruction, and then making decisions about what and how to revise teaching based on these data is referred to as formative evaluation. To meet the requirements of NCLB teachers must be able to use formative evaluation when working with their students.

116

If teachers are going to be required to collect and use data in a meaningful way, then they must be prepared to do so in their teacher-training programs. This means that colleges of education across the country must include specific training in formative evaluation procedures in their preservice courses. The next section briefly discusses implications for school district personnel and teacher trainers.

School District Administrators

Schools districts should have personnel with expertise in progress monitoring. School district personnel can play an important role by (a) encouraging principals to use progress monitoring in their schools; (b) helping the school district to develop progress monitoring systems, bringing in outside experts if necessary; and (c) structuring professional development activities to inservice teachers on such systems.

School Principals

As we mentioned previously, school principals are the instructional leaders in their schools. Thus, they are in a position to ensure that their teachers use progress monitoring systems. If teachers are unwilling or unable to monitor the progress of their students and make instructional decisions based on the data they collect, it is unlikely that students with academic problems will make progress.

Teachers

If teachers are going to be successful in improving the academic achievement of students who are experiencing problems, they must have expertise in (a) developing and using progress monitoring and data collection systems, and (b) matching instruction programs and strategies to students' progress. Teachers need time to acquire skills in data-based progress monitoring systems; therefore, they should take advantage of professional development activities that help them become more efficient and effective in using such systems.

Teacher Trainers

Because NCLB emphasizes accountability and increasing student achievement, it is important that faculty in colleges of education thoroughly prepare preservice teachers to monitor their students' progress and be able to adjust their instructional programs when students are not learning. This approach will require that teacher-training programs offer courses that prepare preservice teachers to monitor students' progress and

117

modify their instructional programs based on the information they collect. Programs should also provide students with ample practice opportunities to develop and refine these skills.

Summary

No Child Left Behind is a complex and controversial law. It is beyond doubt that this law will make profound changes in the ways educators work with students. For the first time, education is accountable for making improvements in students' academic performance. No Child Left Behind points educators toward the tool that will allow schools to make meaningful changes in the academic achievement of their students: scientifically-based research. If the core of our educational practices becomes what the evidence shows us works in teaching, then we can make meaningful changes in our schools.

In our opinion, NCLB is here to stay. Whereas Congress may occasionally tweak the requirements regarding testing and other components, we believe that the major goals of NCLB—the use of scientifically-based and researched educational practices, and holding states, school districts, and schools accountable for increasing student achievement—will be with us for a long time. Mediocre educational results and poor student achievement are no longer just problems—they are now *our* problems.

Discussion Questions

1. How can school district administrators ensure that schools meet the requirements of NCLB?

2. How can principals ensure that schools meet the requirements of NCLB?

3. How can teachers ensure that schools meet the requirements of NCLB?

4. How can colleges of education ensure that schools meet the requirements of NCLB?

5. Does your state have a professional development officer? If so, does he or she base professional development on evidence-based practices?

6. Does your school have a professional development officer? If so, does he or she base professional development on evidence-based practices?

Appendix

Grant Program	Location in NCLB
Local School Improvement grants	Title I, Section 1003(g)
Reading First state grants	Title I, Part B, Subpart1
Early Reading First	Title I, Part B, Subpart 2
Even Start	Title I, Part B, Subpart 3
Improving Literacy Through School Libraries	Title I, Part B, Subpart 4
Education of Migratory Children	Title I, Part C
Prevention and Intervention Programs for Neglected or Delinquent Children or Youth	Title I, Part D
Title I Evaluation and Demonstrations	Title I, Part E, Sections 1501-1503
Close Up Fellowships	Title I, Part E, Sections 1504
Comprehensive School Reform Program	Title I, Part F
Advanced Placement	Title I, Part G
School Dropout Prevention	Title I, Part H
Improving Teacher Quality state grants	Title II, Part A
Mathematics and Science Partnerships	Title II, Part B
Troops to Teachers	Title II, Part C, Subpart 1, Chapter A
Transition to Teaching	Title II, Part C, Subpart 1, Chapter B
National Writing Project	Title II, Part C, Subpart 2
Civic Education	Title II, Part C, Subpart 3
Teaching of Traditional American History	Title II, Part C, Subpart 4
State and Local Technology grants	Title II, Part D, Subpart 1
Ready To Learn Television	Title II, Part D, Subpart 3
Language Instruction for Limited English Proficient and Immigrant Students	Title III
Safe and Drug-Free Schools and Communities	Title IV, Part A
21st Century Community Learning Centers	Title IV, Part B
Innovative Programs state grants	Title V, Part A
Charter Schools	Title V, Part B, Subpart 1
Enhancement Initiatives to Assist Charter School Facility Acquisition, Construction, and Renovation	Title V, Part B, Subpart 2
Voluntary Public School Choice	Title V, Part B, Subpart 3
Magnet Schools Assistance	Title V, Part C
Fund for Improvement of Education	Title V, Part D, Subpart 1
Elementary and Secondary School Counseling programs	Title V, Part D, Subpart 2
Fund for the Improvement of Education (FIE): Character Education	Title V, Part D, Subpart 3

FIE: Smaller Learning Communities	Title V, Part D, Subpart 4
Reading is Fundamental: Inexpensive Book Distribution	Title V, Part D, Subpart 5
FIE: Gifted and Talented Students	Title V, Part D, Subpart 6
FIE: Star Schools	Title V, Part D, Subpart 7
FIE: Ready to Teach	Title V, Part D, Subpart 8
Foreign Language Assistance program	Title V, Part D, Subpart 9
FIE: Carol M. White Physical Education program	Title V, Part D, Subpart 10
FIE: Community Technology Centers	Title V, Part D, Subpart 11
FIE: Educational, Cultural, Apprenticeship, and Exchange Programs For Alaskan Natives, Native Hawaiians, and Their Historical Whaling and Trading Partners in Massachusetts	Title V, Part D, Subpart 12
FIE: Excellence in Economic Education	Title V, Part D, Subpart 13
FIE: Grants to Improve the Mental Health of Children	Title V, Part D, Subpart 14
FIE: Arts in Education	Title V, Part D, Subpart 15
FIE: Parental Assistance and Local Family	Title V, Part D, Subpart 16
FIE: Combating Domestic Violence	Title V, Part D, Subpart 17
FIE: Healthy High-Performance Schools	Title V, Part D, Subpart 18
FIE: Capital Expenses of Providing Equitable Services for Private School Students	Title V, Part D, Subpart 19
FIE: Additional Assistance for Certain Local Educational Agencies Impacted by Federal Property Acquisition	Title V, Part D, Subpart 20
FIE: Women's Educational Equity Act	Title V, Part D, Subpart 21
Grants for State Assessments and Enhanced Assessments	Title VI, Part A, Subpart 1
Flexibility Provisions (Transferability and State and Local Flexibility)	Title VI, Part A, Subpart 2-4
State Flexibility Demonstration program	Title VI, Part A, Subpart 3, Chapter A
Local Flexibility Demonstration program	Title VI, Part A, Subpart 3, Chapter B
Rural Education Initiative	Title VI, Part B
Indian Education	Title VII, Part A
Education of Native Hawaiians	Title VII, Part B
Alaskan Native Education	Title VII, Part C
Impact Aid	Title VIII
Education for Homeless Children and Youth	Title X, Part C
Preparing Tomorrow's Teachers to Use Technology	Title X, Part E

References

Alexander, K., & Alexander, M. D. (2001). *American public school law* (4th ed.). Edina, MN: Thomson/West Publishing Co.

American Federation of Teachers. (1999). *Taking responsibility for ending social promotion: A guide for educators and state and local leaders.* Washington, DC: Author.

Anthes, K. (2002). *No Child Left Behind policy brief: School and district leadership.* Denver: Education Commission of the States. PDF available at www.ecs.org/clearinghouse/32/37/3237.doc

Carnine, D. (2000). *Why education experts resist effective practices: And what it would take to make education more like medicine.* Washington DC: Thomas B. Fordham Foundation.

Coalition for Evidence-Based Policy. (2002). *Bringing evidence-based policy to education: A recommended strategy for the U.S. Department of Education.* Washington, DC: Author. PDF available at http://www.excelgov.org/usermedia/images/uploads/PDFs/CoalitionFinRpt.pdf

Cohen, M. (2002, February). *Assessment and accountability: Lessons from the past, challenges for the future.* Paper presented at a conference sponsored by the Thomas B. Fordham Foundation, No Child Left Behind: What will it take? PDF available at http://www.edexcellence.net/foundation/topic/topic.cfm?topic_id=5

Commission on Excellence in Education. (1983). *A Nation at Risk: An imperative for educational reform.* Washington, DC: Author. Available at http://www.ed.gov/MailingLists/EDInfo/Archive/ msg00022.html

Elliott, J. L., & Thurlow, M. L. (2000). *Improving test performance of students with disabilities...on district and state assessments.* Thousand Oaks, CA: Corwin Press.

Fletcher, J., & Lyon, R. (1998). Reading: A research-based approach. In W. Evers (Ed.), *What's gone wrong in America's classrooms.* Palo Alto, CA: Hoover Institution Press, Stanford University.

Lane, K. K., Gresham, F. M., & O'Shaughnessy, T. E. (2002). *Interventions for children with or at risk for emotional and behavioral disorders.* Boston: Allyn & Bacon.

Learning First Alliance. (2002). *Major changes to ESEA in the No Child Left Behind Act.* Washington, DC: Author. Available at http://www.learningfirst.org

Lyon, G. R.. Speech, Thursday, October 6, 2003. Family Service Guidance Center. Available at CJOnline/Topeka Capital Journal, http://www.cjonline.com/stories/041803/kan_educator.shtml

National Center for Education Statistics. (2001). *Dropout rates in the United States.* http://nces.ed.gov/pubs2002/droppub_2001/ PDF available at http://nces.ed.gov/pubs2002/2002114.pdf

National Center for Education Statistics. (2003). *National Assessment of Educational Progress: The nation's report card.* Washington, DC: Author.

National Reading Panel. (2002). *Teaching children to read: An evidence-based assessment of the scientific research literature on reading and its implications for reading instruction.* Washington, DC: National Institute of Child Development and Human Development.

National Research Council. (2002). *Strategic education research partnerships.* Washington, DC: National Academy Press.

No Child Left Behind, 20 U.S.C. § 6301 et seq.

Paige, R. (2002, November). *Statement of Secretary Paige regarding Title I regulations.* Retrieved August, 2002, from http://www.ed.gov/news/speeches/2002/11/11262002.html?exp=0

Reckase, M. (2002, February). *Using NAEP to confirm state test results: An analysis of issues.* Paper presented at a conference sponsored by the Thomas B. Fordham Foundation, No Child Left Behind: What will it take? PDF available at http://www.edexcellence.net/foundtion/topic/topic.cfm?topic_id=5

U.S. Department of Education. (2002). *No Child Left Behind: A desktop reference.* Washington, DC: Education Publications Center.

Thurlow, M.L., Elliott, J. L., & Ysseldyke, J.E. (2003). *Testing students with disabilities: Practical strategies for complying with district and state requirements.* Thousand Oaks, CA: Corwin Press.

Torgeson, J. (2000). Individual differences in response to early intervention in reading: The lingering problem of treatment resistance. *Learning Disabilities Research and Practice, 15,* 55-64.

Vaughn, S., & Schumm, J.S. (1996). Classroom interactions and inclusion. In D. L. Speech & B. Keogh (Eds.), *Research on classroom ecologies.* Mahwah, NJ: Lawrence Erlbaum.

Whitehurst, G. (2003). *The Institute of Education Sciences: New wine, new bottles.* Presentation at the Annual Conference of the American Educational Research Association. Available at http://www.ed.gov/ print/rschstat/research/pubs/